Beyond the Red Doors

Beyond the Red Doors

Heartfelt Network Marketing

SHAUNA EKSTROM

BEYOND THE RED DOORS

Copyright © 2014 Shauna Ekstrom
All rights reserved.

www.BeyondtheRedDoors.com
www.HeartfeltNetworkMarketing.com

All rights reserved. No part of this publication may be reproduced, stored in a retrieval system, or transmitted, in any form or by any means, electronic, mechanical, photocopying, recording or otherwise, without the prior written permission of the author,

Book cover and illustrations by Bunker Hill Bradley

ISBN: 1514293994
ISBN 13: 9781514293997

Library of Congress Control Number: XXXXX
LCCN Imprint Name: City and State

This book is dedicated ....

To the dreamers

To those who have been afraid to dream.

To those who have stopped dreaming.

To those who are dreaming for the very first time.

And to my father, father-in-law, ex-husband

and my wonderful husband Scott

for teaching me that life is about love of people

and giving with genuine generosity without expecting anything in return.

Testimonials

"Shauna is a beautiful, passionate, and empowering woman. Her presence stays in the mind and lingers in the heart. To know her is to love her."

Grace and Nicki Keohohou
Co-Founders Direct Selling World Alliance
DSWA.org

"Shauna Ekstrom has a huge heart and a passion for the Direct Selling profession. She's helped build an organization on the foundation of patience, seeing other people's strengths and encouraging them to live into their dreams. She dreamed BIG. Through perseverance, love and caring she worked her way into living the dream. Today her inspiring story serves as validation of what's possible. Let Shauna's story inspire you!"

Art Jonak,
MastermindEvent.com Founder and World Class Networker

"Shauna edifies everyone she comes in contact with and feeds their strengths. She has the most gentle, understanding spirit, with a smile that lights up a room. Empowering and helping others achieve success without personal gain is her spirit, and we are thrilled for Shauna's innovative expertise to shine."

Lance and Caroline Dutton

"We met Shauna back in 1999 at the Red Door hair salon. My husband, Dan, and I were instantly attracted to her soft-spoken kindness and gentle spirit. What struck us with Shauna was she came across as a real, living, breathing female version of E. F. Hutton. She was a hairdresser in a quaint little farming and logging community of the Northwest, and when she spoke, we listened. It was compelling. Never pushy or domineering, but always with a quiet voice and a soft suggestion, this sweet woman hypnotized us with her story, and before we knew what happened, we had enrolled more than eighty people in her business in about three weeks. Shauna will do whatever it takes to get it done and again in such a sweet, easy way. She is a survivor and is always positive. What an amazingly positive attitude she keeps even when something seems impossible. She has the warmest and most fun heart of anyone we know, and she can be silly, fun, and amazingly successful all at the same time. We are so grateful to have Shauna as a friend!"

Shelley and Dan Morgado

"Shauna Ekstrom's story is one of the most courageous and inspirational adventures of our profession. And from all of her challenges and triumphs has come true Mastery. Mastery of believing in others even when they don't see or believe in themselves. And Mastery of leading and coaching them along their own path to greatness. I love this story. I love this book.

Richard Bliss Brooke
Owner, BlissBusiness.com
Author, Mach II *and* The Four Year Career

"I'm a passionate believer in true relationship marketing - it's about focusing on connecting authentically from the heart, coming from a place of true service, adding value, and genuinely caring about the success of the people in your network. Shauna Ekstrom certainly embodies all this and more; she's a masterful relationship builder. It's a joy to see her sharing her journey and secrets of success in her new book!"

Mari Smith
Social Media Thought Leader
Top Facebook Marketing Expert

"Success always comes from within, but there are always outside influences, and I am honored to think that I was in her life at a critical time for her. It has been amazing to see Shauna grow into the beautiful and amazing person that she has become. Early on she dug herself out of a very bad situation and began believing in herself and saw the need in other people, and she has been on a crusade to help them ever since.

Zig says, 'You can have anything in life you want, if you just help enough other people get what they want.' The evidence is in; Shauna has accomplished that and continues to do just that. Love her so much and proud of all her accomplishments."

Stan Barker

Foreword

Shauna Ekstrom has lived a very interesting life! In Beyond the Red Doors, she freely shares her life's experiences, exhibiting an unusual transparency rarely found in publication.

Have you ever wondered why some people who grow up in difficult circumstances somehow overcome to achieve more than many of the more privileged, while others (in both categories) appear to give up on themselves – and often others – so early in life? Shauna is among those who used her early challenges to develop attitudes and skills that opened for her the doors to success. She learned as a girl to work hard and to be persistent in her efforts, and she carried these qualities with her into adulthood and eventually into building her very successful network marketing business. The good news for you is her story will give you the direction and encouragement you need to open your own doors, regardless of your past circumstances.

Shauna Ekstrom has developed "Heartfelt Network Marketing" which is, in my opinion, a unique business concept, one that could and probably should be adapted to most business efforts. In Beyond the Red Doors, Shauna explains both the concept and the application, all the time encouraging the incorporation of the principles into virtually any industry.

As "they" say, the proof is in the pudding. The "heartfelt" mindset is taking hold across America as our society returns to customer-centered business relationships. Shauna's story is well-written and speaks to all of us who seek to improve our relationships – business and personal.

Tom Ziglar
CEO-Proud Son of Zig Ziglar

Table of Contents

Introduction	1
Section I	**7**
Through the Red Doors	7
Section II	**59**
The Dawn of Heartfelt Network Marketing	59
The Principals of Heartfelt Marketing	60
Heartfelt Dreaming, Hope, and the Ugly Alternative	77
The Fundamentals of the Network Marketing Industry	101
Network Marketing Myths	113
This Is a Heartfelt Honorable Profession	121
Personal Development	145
Belief in Yourself, Your Product, and Your Company	185
Section III	**199**
Building Your Business	199
The Core Steps to Building Your Business	200
Recruiting	203
Heartfelt Network Marketing Is a Storytelling Business	205
Creating Mutually Rewarding Relationships	211
Tapping into Technology	228
Attracting People to You	232
Having Fun on the Way	235
Section IV	**238**
Reference Materials	239
Disclaimer	240

Introduction

The summer after we finished second grade, my best friend Jill and I started a business. We sold lemonade on the steps of the neighborhood church. After a few weeks, we expanded into food service with the invention of Fruitios. This wistful concoction was produced by pouring Jell-O over Cheerios and cutting it into little blocks. Business was booming, so naturally, we went retail. Jill and I would collect useless knickknacks from our storage rooms and sheds, clean them up, and sell these "treasures" to our friends.

This entrepreneurial spirit kept us going all the way to the end of sixth grade, when my family moved to a different town. The culmination of our joint venture was a tour of our working-class neighborhood that we put together for the kids from the "right side of the tracks." We made a map, set up the itinerary, and even came up with a product placement—the Candy Machine, which was located in an industrial office complex. The kids taking the tour were told to bring their dimes for a surprise treat. We really gave a boost to our local economy that day…well, at the very least, the owner of that candy machine had quite a windfall.

Recently, I was talking with an old girlfriend of mine who reminded me of my early experiments in the business world. It made me take stock of my life and look at the road that got me where I am today—a proud, independent, successful business owner with a dedicated team of more than 110,000 associates. The thing that intrigued me most was that it took me more than ten years of developing and working various network marketing businesses to reach the coveted six-figure-income bracket, but it only took me two years after that to reach the millionaire category. I asked myself why growing my business since then has seemed effortless, and the answer, when it came to me, sounds almost too simple to be true—heart. After ten years of trying to sell products and services, I learned that it's the heartfelt relationships you form with your clients and team members that push and pull you to that next level.

This book is the journey that brought me from being a small-town hairdresser to a millionaire in the network marketing arena. It's about how I developed a way of doing business that builds bridges and connections instead of burning them. I call this my Heartfelt Network Marketing way. Whether you are a novice or a veteran networker, this book will help you grow personally and professionally while teaching you how to build a stronger, more dedicated team. After all, network marketing is all about personal growth. You can't grow your team unless you yourself are growing. Remember: your first recruit is you.

I do not intend for this book to be a "get rich quick" guide. Instead, it is a heartfelt look at the network marketing business and a template for living a fuller and more joyful life as a networker. The principles I put forth in the coming chapters focus on people and relationships rather than numbers and compensation plans. What I have learned, and what I want to pass on to you, my readers, is that in this profession, the money nearly always follows the relationships.

There are many traditional network marketing methods and tools that I use simply because they are necessary if I want to be successful, and there are just as many that I have abandoned or modified to suit my sharing and caring approach to recruiting and building the business.

This book concentrates on the heartfelt way and is not meant to be a comprehensive book on the world of network marketing. There are thousands of wonderful network marketing resources available to you, and I encourage you to consult these as well as books on personal development. Network marketing is all about personal growth, and we believe that you can't grow a business or other people if you are not growing yourself.

Having said that, network marketing is a real business, and becoming a successful professional networker requires dedication, time, and *heart work*. This level of commitment will have an effect on your current lifestyle, but it will have a far greater impact on your future lifestyle.

My intent is to help you go further and faster in your business than I ever have. We advance on the backs of those who came before us, and I take pride in being able to offer advice to the next wave of entrepreneurs. In the following chapters, I will discuss a few challenges that are common to all business ventures and some that are specific to network marketing. I will also talk about how learning to overcome these challenges allowed me to live a fuller, happier life.

Perhaps you have read success stories and seen photos of top achievers draped across the front of their exotic sports cars, and maybe your thoughts looked something like these:

- If only I could sell.
- If only I had the nerve.
- If only I weren't shy.
- If only I could overcome rejection.
- If only I had the time.
- If only I had the network.
- If only I had the money.
- If only I knew how to do it.
- If only I had someone to do this with.

You may be surprised to know that a lot of us had some or all of the same concerns just before we started our network marketing careers. Truthfully, there is no easy button, but there are many ways to overcome these challenges, and some of them disappear altogether when you follow the Heartfelt Network Marketing way.

The Heartfelt Network Marketing way is an alternative to the hard-sell approach. It comes from your heart first and then your pocketbook. There are three "if only" challenges to overcome:

- If only I believed in myself.
- If only I knew why I want a successful network marketing business.
- If only I had a story.

The most important question to ask yourself is why you want to build your own successful business. I entered network marketing because I wanted freedom to live life on my own terms, including financial freedom and an alternative to my physically crippling career as a hair stylist. My physiotherapist had told me that I had to give up my job because I only had a few years before I would do irreparable damage to my back. I saw network marketing as the most viable option for a woman in her forties who was drowning in bills, working long hours day and night, and having very little free time to spend with her family or see the outside world.

This book consists of three sections:

- Through the Red Doors: This is my personal story of how I started life on the wrong side of the tracks and how, through dreaming, hard work, and determination, I achieved the freedom and the finances to live life the way I want to live it.

- The Dawn of Heartfelt Marketing: This is where you will learn the principals of Heartfelt Network Marketing.

    - Your dream
    - What is Heartfelt Network Marketing to you?
    - Your honorable profession
    - Your personal development
    - Your four key beliefs

- Building Your Business:

    - Creating mutually rewarding relationships
    - It is a storytelling business
    - Having fun
    - Tapping into technology
    - Attracting people to you
    - Recruiting

Working out why you are entering network marketing is the first step. Knowing why at the outset will help you read this book with intention. If you have your why firmly plugged into your subconscious, you will automatically seek out the advice that works best for your plan, and you will start to work out how best to apply it. Knowing what your intention is before you start an endeavor is powerful, and it will reward you immeasurably.

Section I

Through the Red Doors

I Did This,

and

You Can Too!

How I went from very humble beginnings as a child of the fifties to millionaire is an interesting story, and if you had asked me how it happened before I wrote this book, I would have attributed it to my hunger to be free and the belief that there was a way to get there. However, writing this book has forced me to take a long, hard look at my journey, and I now realize that it took a lot more than hunger and belief. They are certainly the key drivers; however, many other supporting factors helped me to finally live my dream of living instead of longing.

I have come a long way from being a teenage mom, drowning in debt and stress. My children are all grown up and creating wonderful lives of their own, and I have the time and the resources to enjoy my three beautiful granddaughters in ways that I never had with my own children. My daughter, Heidi, is carrying on the family networking business and reached the six-figure-income mark a lot faster than I did. Justin and Nathan are young men living in Houston, and I am married to an amazing man, Dr. Scott Peterson. Life is great, and I wake up every morning excited about the possibilities the day will bring. Every day, network marketing gives us the opportunity to pay it forward and help change hundreds of people's lives for the better. We are forever grateful that we are in the network marketing profession.

Over the years, I have never stopped dreaming, and now Scott and I are working on a new set of dreams together. I have to admit that having a husband who is as excited about network marketing and life as I am is a dream I never dared to dream.

Looking back, I can truly say that I had a wonderful childhood. Growing up in the fifties was a lot simpler and I think a lot less stressful than the world our children and grandchildren are subjected to today. We were free to run and explore our little world without fear, and our imaginations created everything we needed to have fun with our friends. Our focus was on today, and the future was something we caught glimpses of in black and white on TV.

My earliest recollection is of skinny-dipping in the creek next to the little old farmhouse we lived in. I was around three years old. My days were filled with running after my older sister across the wheat fields, laughing and squealing with our yellow Lab called Snow Boy. Living on the farm in Lorenzo, Idaho, was one of my father's dreams, but while we kids were blissfully unaware of any trouble, I believe his dream turned into a financial nightmare; the next thing I knew, we were living in a trailer park. I loved the trailer just as much as the farm, and I couldn't imagine why anyone wouldn't want to live in a brand-new trailer house with pink appliances and the cutest curtains.

On the socioeconomic scale, our family may have been considered poor, but if we were, I wasn't aware of it until much later. Mom was a stay-at-home mom like most other moms in those days, and Dad was a very hardworking man. He started out driving tankers, but my fondest memories are from the time when he was a Trailways bus driver in Salt Lake City. Sometimes we would go with him and listen to the great stories he would tell everyone along the way. All the passengers loved him because he was so much fun and his storytelling always made the trip seem faster and more interesting.

By the time I was seven, we were living in a little cottage across from my grandma's in Swede Town, Utah. It was a small burg in the north end of Salt Lake City originally settled by a group of Swedish immigrants and surrounded by industrial refineries and a sand and gravel pit. It was only about six square blocks, but it was big enough for me.

Moving into town and starting school was exciting, but it was also when I started to realize that not everyone is considered equal or the same. To start with, we belonged to a different religion than most of the other families in our area, and that meant that we went to our own meetings and social events.

I started school in Swede Town in second grade and met my soon-to-be best friend, Jill, on the first day. My teacher Miss Shields taught kindergarten through second grade in a one-room schoolhouse. Recess was my favorite thing about school because for fifteen minutes I could run around with the other kids screaming with laughter and having fun, and the down side of school for me was class time, which felt like being in a prison. Sitting still in class didn't interest me, so I would tune out and begin day dreaming about escaping the classroom's four walls and being outside, free to explore and have fun. It's strange, but for the first time I just realized that escaping four walls has been a recurring dream of mine since I was a child, and I had thought it was only since I'd been working in the Red Door Hair Salon.

School never got any easier for me, and when I was around thirteen years old, I started to sleep a lot, both in and out of class. I remember coming home from school, going to bed with books on my lap, and waking up that way in the morning. I'd skip dinner a lot of times, and Mom would just come to my room and pull the covers up over me. We didn't know it at the time, but I had developed narcolepsy. I only know about it now because when my eldest son was in his teens, he was diagnosed with narcolepsy, and I learned that it is hereditary. It's a chronic neurological disorder caused by the brain's inability to regulate sleep-wake cycles. To this day, I can go straight into the REM sleep stage within minutes, and I have no control over it. The trick is to keep the brain stimulated, and elementary school just didn't do it for me; consequently, everyone thought I was just a sleepy, disinterested child who could flip from hyperactive to hibernation in the blink of an eye.

Although I was bored in the classroom, I loved going to school, because there were always lots of other kids to have fun with. I wasn't in the cool group, but I was a sweet and happy child, so I always had friends. I liked everyone and was always happy to play with anyone. I loved listening to others' stories.

After school, it was not unusual to see a homeless man sitting on our porch waiting patiently for some of Mom's home cooking. We lived near the railway, and drifters with their heads bowed would tap on our door and ask for help. Mom and Grandma never turned anyone away, and they would cook up whatever we had left in the cupboards. I never tired of seeing these poor men light up with joy when mom handed them a plate of freshly cooked eggs and bacon, with thick buttered toast and a wax milk carton full of hot coffee. Without a doubt, my lifelong passion for helping people started on our porch as I watched the faces of these poor, helpless men light up when they saw that someone cared. Even for someone as young as I was at the time, it was easy to see the positive impact a little help can give someone in need.

Sometimes, Jill and I would follow the homeless to the place where they slept and generally hung out. They had little caves and holes in the side of the hill where they slept, and Jill named it the Bum Hole, which didn't impress our moms too much. It was a great source of adventure for us as we poked around for hours discovering little things we could add to our stockpile of treasures. We would shriek with excitement when we found an old bent spoon that they had used, or a tin can that they'd actually eaten out of.

From time to time, my father brought home families who couldn't afford a motel and would otherwise have to sleep in the bus depot overnight waiting for their next connection. Mom would make up beds for them and he would get them back to the depot early the next day. Dad was very generous and giving to all who were less fortunate. I also remember packing up our hand-me-down clothes and leaving them on the porch of a family of kids we knew from school who were less fortunate; we always made sure they were not home when we dropped off the boxes so they never knew who left the clothes.

Seeing firsthand how hard it can get for some people and how a little caring and kindness can lift their spirits are experiences that will be with me forever, and I thank my mom, dad, and grandma from my heart for teaching me that and showing me their love for humanity.

Jill and I were joined at the hip, and after school we spent countless hours exploring and creating our own exciting version of the world. Climbing trees and building tree houses was one of our favorite games. We built them in different parts of town, and sometimes we even did our homework up among the branches. We saw ourselves as adventurers, and one time we discovered a way to get to the rooftop of an old storefront. This became my special place to dream. I spent many hours sitting up there looking across at the rooftops, dreaming of what the world must be like and thinking about how one day I would work out how to go see it for myself. I loved being up high and looking out, and the higher I got, the happier I would be, because the houses and walls became smaller and I could see beyond my little patch of the world.

Jill and I were more than explorers; we were also budding entrepreneurs. During summer break, we set up a little stand on the church steps and sold homemade lemonade and a delightful treat of our own creation: we poured Jell-O over Cheerios, and when it was set we cut it into little blocks and called them Fruitios.

The concept of multiple sources of income is the hallmark of an entrepreneur, and even at that young age, Jill and I were onto it. Over time, we realized that we had to expand our product range if we were going to keep our customers coming back. We figured that the other kids were just like us and probably wanted treasures just like we did. We raided our parents' sheds and asked our moms for anything they didn't want, like used lipsticks, makeup, or earrings—absolutely anything would do. The kids loved our expansion program, and we loved them, but we were in business, and if the kids didn't have enough money, we would send them home to rob their piggy banks. We were pretty tough too, because at times when they'd come back and still didn't have quite enough money, we'd tell them to go home and try again, reminding them that it only cost a nickel. Just recently, I was visiting with an old school friend and she reminded me of the time I used to send her home to empty her piggy bank so she could buy a treasure from our stall. These are heartfelt memories that make up the fabric of our lives.

Jill and I never stood still for long; our next business venture was tourism. We believed that we lived in the most exciting place in the world, and we thought of ourselves as the unofficial Swede Town tourism authority. We created a map of our neighborhood that highlighted our special places, including our three treehouses, the abandoned house we could get into through the window, the Bum Hole, and the candy machine in the transport office. We were so enthusiastic about our tour that we convinced a group of school friends who lived on the right side of the tracks in Ensign Downs to travel to Swede Town and take a tour. They started the tour by catching the city bus to Swede Town, which was exciting for them because they were used to riding the regular yellow school bus; of course, we pointed out that we got to ride the city bus all the time. We all had such great fun following our map through town, and like all great tours, we saved the best for last—the candy machine. We had advised our customers ahead of time to bring their dimes so they could buy candy from the machine in an office in an industrial park area which we used to call the Candy Store. We had the time of our lives, and everyone went home happy and high on sugar.

Growing up with Jill was wonderful. But one day, midway through junior high, everything changed. My father bought a two-thousand-square-foot home on the hill, and we had to pack up our lives and leave our old two-bedroom, one-bath cottage to move to what my parents called a better part of town. I adjusted to my new school well enough, but there was nothing truly memorable about it. I had left my heart and my enthusiasm for adventure in Swede Town. Two long years later, I was excited to learn that we were moving back to our little cottage across from Grandma's in Swede Town, and I couldn't wait.

I was now in the ninth grade and extremely excited about being with Jill and all my other old friends again. It never occurred to me that things would be any different than when we had left two years earlier, but sadly everything had changed. Two years is a lifetime when you are a child; all my friends had moved on with their lives. We were all young teenagers now, and climbing trees and exploring was replaced by other activities.

Jill wanted to include me; she invited me to be with her new friends, but I didn't have anything in common with them. Her new friends came from a more affluent area, and I quickly became aware that I was not a part of their group. Sadly, it wasn't long before I stopped joining them. Jill and I were still friends, but our friendship never felt quite the same again. I just didn't fit in anymore, and like most kids, I wanted to be like everyone else. For me, it wasn't going to happen for quite a few years…decades, in fact.

Now that I was in my teens, I started to understand more about what it meant when my parents told me we couldn't afford this or that. My father always wanted us to have more than he had, and when I asked him for a dime to go to the movies, he would always give me a dollar. I would tell him that I only needed ten cents, but he would say, "I don't want you kids to ever watch other kids have an apple, and you can't have one. I wanted an apple so much when I was a little kid, and we couldn't afford it, and I never want you kids to go without." He was always about giving us whatever he had, and he was generous with everything he had…and didn't have. One of the more curious aspects of my childhood was that in spite of our money woes, dad always drove a nice car. Looking back, I suppose driving his beautiful car was his one and only escape where he could dream.

It was around this time that I became sensitive and started to notice and place importance on how I looked compared to my peers, especially when it came to clothes. I was a teenager, and what you wore was important. Mom had always sewn beautiful dresses for my sister and me by hand, but in my mind quality wasn't the issue, it was the difference between homemade and store-bought. Looking like the other teenage girls was important to me, and I never got there. Fitting in was becoming harder every day, and it constantly weighed on my mind. No matter what I did, I never seemed to fit in with the other girls, and I knew it was only going to get worse when school started again because I didn't have any new clothes to wear. I had just turned fifteen, and the thought of going into tenth grade wearing last year's clothes just terrified me. Jill and her mom had been getting her ready all summer long. They weren't rich either, but her mom worked at JCPenney in the sewing department, and she allowed Jill to pick the most up-to-date styles and material, and together they sewed dresses for every school day of the month. Unfortunately, Mom and Dad had a stressful summer that year. There was a lot of emotional turmoil, and it was so bad I worried they might get divorced. Under these circumstances, there was no way I was going to add to the upset by asking for new store-bought clothes just for school. However, I was not prepared to go back to school in last year's handmade clothes, which were now out of date and way too small.

Just when I thought the rest of my life was over, our next-door neighbor showed me a possible way out of my dilemma. Over the summer, I had been babysitting for her children, and she told me that she had been to beauty school. It sounded great. We had one in town, and Mom had taken me there a couple of times for cheap haircuts. The girls always looked like they were having lots of fun. I called the school and found out that I could start at sixteen, and the best thing of all was that we all wore the same cute little white uniform. I don't know exactly how I did it, but I convinced my parents to let me drop out of high school and enroll in beauty school. I was only fifteen at the time, and I couldn't start until my sixteenth birthday, so for four miserable months I continued to babysit and got a temporary telemarketing job with Arthur Murray's Ballroom Dance School. I was on my way and not looking back.

I started beauty school the day after my sixteenth birthday. My parents paid the seventy-five-dollar tuition fee, and I thought I would be able to repay them from the tips I earned doing people's hair while being trained. I was even able to get a free uniform, because the school ran a competition that I won, and first prize was a brand-new uniform. I finally felt comfortable in my own skin, and even though I was shy, I looked forward to mixing with other girls because I figured that with my uniform I looked just as good as they did. We were all learning the same things, and more importantly, we were all dressed alike.

Even though school had been difficult for me, I discovered that learning was easy if I was interested in the subject. I wasn't worried about beauty school, because I was hungry to learn and I had a natural creative flair—I just needed to be shown what to do.

Turning sixteen was a pivotal year for me; not only did I transition from being a junior high school kid to a trainee beautician, but I started dating Virgil, who was to become my first husband and father of our three children. Virgil was related to Linda, the neighbor I babysat for, and she was very involved in her church. Often I would help Linda out with the kids at her church coop events, and it was there that Virgil first noticed me. Later on, he told me that when he first saw me at one of these events he said to himself that he was going to marry me, which was amazing because we hadn't even met and I didn't know he even existed.

Over the following months, he started dropping into Linda's on the weekends, and eventually he asked me out. The attraction was mutual; I was fifteen going on twenty, with big hair, heavy makeup, and false eyelashes, and he was twenty-six and drove a cool, red Torino with a white racing stripe. I can still picture that car in my mind as if it was yesterday. I was so young and impressionable, and he was so grown up and cool; it didn't take much persuasion on his behalf. Years later, I learned that my dad told Mom that I had fallen in love with the Torino and not Virgil, and that I was too young to date. In hindsight he was probably right on both counts, but I was a girl in a hurry to grow up. Mom thought Dad was being ridiculous; she was convinced that I seriously loved Virgil. He was ten years older than me and much like a very kind, fatherly figure. I felt very secure with Virgil, especially since my parents were struggling with their marriage at the time.

It's funny what you learn years later. I wonder if I would have made different choices had I known what my parents were thinking. Virgil and I broke up several times, but that cool car kept bringing us back together, and it was fun to be treated like an adult. We dated all through beauty school and married after graduation, when I turned seventeen. I did say I was in a hurry, and with childlike enthusiasm I couldn't wait to be a mom. Heidi was born when I was eighteen, and then three years later Justin came into the world via our bathroom floor.

It was during my beauty school training that I met my first mentor, Gene Herrera. Gene was a wonderful hair stylist and a very astute businessman. Always on the lookout for fresh, young talent for his salons, he judged the beauty school competitions, He was also a fierce competitor who won many major hair styling competitions himself. It was Gene who introduced me to the competitive side of hair styling. He gave me my first ticket to a competition, and I immediately fell in love with the excitement of competing and the chance to learn from incredibly talented, award-winning hair stylists. I found the whole experience fun and motivating. Gene encouraged me to enter competitions even though I had not yet graduated, and thanks to his coaching I won several trophies before leaving beauty school.

I was six months into my training when Gene asked me to work for him in his salon as soon as I graduated. Beauty school was one of the happiest times of my life. I had the chance to be creative, I fit in with everyone else, I was hungry to learn, and I had an amazing mentor who was genuinely interested in helping me be the best I could be.

As soon as I graduated from beauty school, I joined Gene's salon. He knew the importance of having award-winning hair stylists in his salon. He constantly encouraged all of us to compete and mentored me to get into the state competition. The idea that I had just graduated and now I was competing at the state level was crazy, but he supplied the model and worked with me all the way. He wanted all of us to get ahead and was always giving us free tickets to hair shows. I could never understand why I was the only one who would go. It was inspiring, and I loved it. I loved the whole art of it. He was an amazing artist, and I just loved being around him and learning from him and the other artists at the competitions.

Working in Gene's salon was not all competitions and fun. It was also my first real job, and I had to build my own clientele. I didn't know it at the time, but this was how it would be for the rest of my life. I have always been directly responsible for my take home pay, and I can't even imagine what it must be like to be guaranteed a salary regardless of how I performed.

I was still a teenager, and I was shy and awkward when it came to speaking to people. Thank goodness for Gene; he had it all worked out. He taught me the value of advertising and promotion. He made up some flyers announcing that an award-winning stylist, Shauna Wilson, was coming to Entre Hair Fashions, and my brother Dean and I delivered them all over the neighborhood. People started coming into the salon, and we gave them a good deal if they asked for Shauna. His strategy worked from the get-go, and he generously displayed my trophies right next to his…and he had a lot of trophies.

Gene taught me so much about customer service and going the extra mile. He explained the value of giving great service regardless of whether I was paid or not. We were all on commission, and we didn't get paid for shampoos, but he had me shampoo as many of his clients as I could squeeze in, explaining that when he was too busy his clientele would ask for me, and he was right. I put my heart and soul into those free shampoos, and it wasn't long before his clients started coming to me when he was booked out or away.

In a very short time, I went from zero to booked solid, regularly bringing in fifty to seventy dollars a day. This rise didn't happen by accident. I listened to everything Gene had to say, and more importantly, I did it. I couldn't get enough of it, and often when I had a spare few minutes I would sweep the salon floor just so I could watch him work with his clients. The other girls checked into the salon when they had appointments, whereas I was there from seven o'clock in the morning to seven at night…or later if clients wanted me to stay. I would agree to whatever time my client wanted, and I would be there when people walked in off the street without an appointment. Most days, I would see more than twenty clients at $2.50 a haircut. The hours didn't worry me, because I loved every minute of it and couldn't believe I was being paid to make twenty or more people happy every single day. The feeling of happiness I would get when my clients' faces lit up when they saw their new look was wonderful.

I was so hungry to succeed that I consciously worked at overcoming my shyness. Watching Gene and the other girls, I realized that it didn't pay to be shy. I also learned that I needed to be an entertainer as well as a stylist. In fact, it seemed that being a great listener and making people laugh was on top of the list. There was one particular stylist who was just terrible at her job. Her clients were forever coming to us to have little things fixed, and rather than complain about her they would make excuses for her and keep on going back. They loved her personality and she was hilarious. This was a great lesson in life for me. I learned that being a great person to be around is just as important as doing a great job. I also started to understand that people didn't always come into the salon to get a perfect haircut. They came for therapy, to escape, to be entertained—they came for lots of different reasons. This started my lifelong interest in psychology and understanding people.

Sadly, the downside of my rapid rise to successful hair stylist in Gene's salon was the reaction from the other stylists. As my client list grew, so did the wall between me and the other girls, and that old feeling of not fitting in raised its ugly head again. I was the junior and the other girls were in their twenties, thirties, and forties, and within six months, I was making more money than them. They started making fun of me and calling me Gene's pet, and the terror I had felt at being an outcast throughout my high school years came back with a vengeance. Even though I loved being mentored by Gene and he made me feel like an award-winning hair stylist, the emotional trauma I experienced from the girls was too much for me, so I left. I was still a teenager, and the only option I could see was to run; so that's what I did.

I left Gene's vibrant, exciting studio and incredible mentoring to work with a woman who had a small home salon. I convinced myself that it was a good move because it was closer to our little house, but deep down I knew I just wanted to hide and get on with my art. My need to blend in with the crowd had overpowered my hunger to learn and grow, but not for long. Unfortunately, my boss and I worked opposite hours, so I had no one to learn from, and after a year of doing the same ladies at the same time every week, I felt like I was living in a soap opera. I had to leave, but I wasn't ready to go back to a salon and work with a bunch of catty women.

I was still very young and hungry to learn and be creative, so rather than face a new group of stylists in another salon, I decided to start my own home salon. By this time, I had been working for a couple of years, and my clientele had happily followed me from one location to the next, so I knew that I would continue to have customers. Though I found that it was very difficult to get ahead financially, because my clients would pay me what they could afford, and they were in the same financial fix that we were in.

I was stuck between a rock and a hard place yet again. My friend Polly suggested that I try getting into a big-time popular salon in town where everyone was doing well, which would allow me to make more money. It was called Sunday Morning, and it was the happening salon in Bountiful at the time. I had matured a little by now and was not so worried about what other people thought about me, and more importantly, I needed to make more money. Virgil was driving a truck by now, but sadly workers at his company were going on strike, which meant even less money than usual. At this point, Justin was six months old and Heidi was three and a half, and finally the financial stress of supporting our young family gave me the push I needed to get back into a salon. I met with Dorothy Ewing, the owner of Sunday Morning, and fortunately she hired me right away.

The hippie era had arrived since I had last worked in a commercial salon, and it brought with it a hairstyling revolution. Young men and boys were wearing their hair long and had switched from their old barbers to hair salons. They trusted us to listen to what they wanted and not cut their long locks off before they had a chance to sit down. At the same time, women started getting blow-dry hairstyling rather than their weekly wash and set. It was exciting; we now had men and women coming into salons, and they wanted us to experiment and be creative.

I was no longer shy with women, but now I had a whole new type of clientele: teenage boys. Even though I had been styling for four years and was the mother of two children, I was still only twenty-one, and talking to teenage boys and young men was not something that I had ever experienced before now. I had no idea how to talk to them, so I did what I have always done. I asked someone who looked like she knew what she was doing. I asked Marie Cook, and she was wonderful. "All you need to do is ask them questions about their sports teams and what kinds of sports they are into, and they will do the rest," she suggested. This was a revelation to me. To get both the boys and myself comfortable, all I had to do was ask questions about their interests and they would talk, and I would listen while cutting their hair.

This whole hair revolution was fascinating, and I saw it as a new and exciting art form. I was inspired again, and I started going to even more hair shows than ever before. I noticed that every time I created an amazing new style I'd learned at a hair show, I would get a flush of new clients. This was another valuable lesson: if you're not growing, getting new clients and new referrals, you're going backward.

My hairstyling career was going great, but our family life was not doing so well. My husband was a hardworking man who had always worked for a church cooperative; their focus was to grow the church holdings. The workers, in turn, regardless of their profession or education, never made enough to live on. The mind-set was to give everything to the church and your personal needs would be taken care of, but the truth was, most members suffered both economically and emotionally. Personal needs and "extras" were considered frivolous and pretentious, and it was deemed honorable to suffer for the cause rather than to have personal prosperity. I was a young mother who wanted more for her family than the crumbs handed out by the cooperative. I had energy and drive, and I knew that I could work as hard and as often as necessary to move our family ahead, but this was a total contradiction to my husband's belief system.

I wanted to dress my two little ones in the latest cute clothes and have some nice little things in our home to make it homier. I suppose I thought that maybe we could buy our way into belonging by having some of the same things as everyone around us. This sounds naïve, but at the time I was still a child with no experience in raising a family, running a household, or handling money, let alone managing the philosophical gap between Virgil's beliefs and mine. I had lived at home with my parents until the day I married Virgil, so I had no experience being an adult in an adult world, and it wasn't long before our credit card debt was way out of our control. My husband and I thought that longer hours, later nights, earlier mornings, and an extra day would fix the debt, but unfortunately our idealistic solution was never going to solve the problem. It sounds silly now, but it never occurred to me to curb my spending. In fact, to make things worse, when we felt despair over the debt we would fix things by going out to dinner and spending more money. I looked like a grown woman with my big hair and makeup, but I saw the world through the inexperienced eyes of a teenager. Unfortunately, it was this inexperience of the real world and not knowing that everything can't be fixed by going shopping that kept us chained to the financial stress wheel for years to come.

I loved being a mom, especially the baby stages, and even though I worked long hours, I tried to spend as much time as possible with Heidi and Justin. I raised them with spiritual values, and we attended meetings two to three times a week. Often Virgil worked nights and afternoon shifts, so I had a lot of time to do things alone with the children. One of my favorite things was to put them in a stroller and walk down to the city park. I'd buy tacos or cheeseburgers or whatever I could pick up at the little Mexican restaurant in Bountiful, and we would sit in the park and eat dinner. It was simple but so enjoyable.

Although I love my children with all my heart, I truly never felt that I was prepared to be a parent. I knew that being the best mom possible was the most important job I would ever have, and I was desperate for help, so in the early years I would ask everyone for their opinion, especially my friend Polly. Whatever Polly said, I would do—which meant I was stricter with the kids than I naturally would have been. Later on I started taking parenting classes, because I felt that I needed professional help. I was raised in a typical '50s household where children were taught to be seen and not heard. That was the normal behavior for the '50s child but not so much the '70s child. My daughter and son were brilliant and challenged me at every turn. They were precocious and I was worried about how they might grow up. The parenting classes were once a week for six weeks, and the instructor was Bert Chamberlain, a wonderful licensed psychologist with a great sense of humor. Bert explained that parents were no match for kids and that kids have no rules or boundaries, while we do. I became fascinated with the psychological complexities of people, and his insights helped me so much that I took the six-week class seven times.

Through these parenting classes, I started to look closer at my marriage, because we were not having the best of times. About eighteen months into our marriage, Virgil had quit working for his church cooperative and started driving for a trucking company in an attempt to earn more money for the family. This was a terrible emotional burden for him, because he wasn't ready to enter into a world he didn't know or understand. Our marriage was not coping well with the combination of Virgil's emotional stress and my feelings of inadequacy. We needed some serious help, so I started using some of Bert's parenting strategies in my marriage, and they seemed to work. This was encouraging. I asked Bert if he also did marriage counseling, and he said yes, so at that point, Virgil and I started our marriage counseling era.

I think I have always been interested in books that had to do with people. I called it psychology, but I think it was more about anything to do with positive thinking. I dealt with people and children every day, and by 1997, two of my own kids were in their twenties and the youngest was still an adolescent, and I wanted to understand them more. I came across a great book titled *Please Understand Me*, by David Keirsey. It is a psychology book that focuses on personality types and characteristics, and it contains a great personality questionnaire. Not only did I use it personally, but I used it in the salon with my clients. Sometimes there would be a group of women waiting or just visiting, and they would do the test. Then they'd laugh and talk about it with each other while I was doing hair. I felt it lifted people, and if it helped them as well, that was a bonus.

I was always reading books on positive thinking and telling my clients about what I had learned, suggesting that they too should get a copy. Often I would buy extra copies of a great book and give them out as gifts. It sounds a bit like network marketing doesn't it? But at the time I had no idea my reading and passion for helping people was going to lead me to a new, exciting world.

When my first two children were in junior high and high school, I wanted them to experience a different lifestyle, so we moved to the Northwest. Within that next year, we had a wonderful addition to the family, my youngest son, Nathan. We eventually ended up in a small town called Enumclaw, located about forty-five miles southeast of Seattle, Washington. It is absolutely beautiful and is the "Gateway" to the north entrance to Mt. Rainier.

Just like a lot of families, we never seemed to have enough money or time to have fun, but it was not all doom and gloom. For the next several years, I could escape every day to my salon Hair by Shauna, which was in a separate part of our home. As I have said, I consider hairstyling to be an art form, and I was passionate about the creative side of hair. Every day, someone new would walk into my salon, and I would be given the opportunity to not only help them look beautiful on the outside but also feel better about themselves on the inside. I believed that hairstyling was a win-win situation—I felt great when I saw the wonderful change in my clients' confidence and self-esteem, and they felt happy and confident enough to reach inside and let others see their inner beauty. If you are a hair stylist, aesthetician, personal trainer, life coach, teacher, or caring friend, never underestimate the positive impact on someone that a little change here and there can make. I have always felt that natural is way overrated and beauty can be bought and taught. It was my daily interaction with my hair salon clients that fired up my passion for understanding people and psychology. I have found that not all change has to be earth shattering or stressful. Sometimes all it takes is someone to listen and care or for another person to say he or she believes in you. I loved my hairstyling career because it was creative and there was something new every day, but mostly I loved making a positive difference in people's lives. Making men and women feel understood, prettier, and giving them a place to come where someone really listened was heartwarming for me and my clients.

I met so many wonderful people while doing hair, and one of my dearest friends started out as a client at my home salon. Joni owned a diet center, and we got along so well that she would make her appointments for the end of the day so we could spend time together after I finished her hair. Over the years, our children got to know each other and we became family friends.

Joni and I worked long hours and didn't have time for girly lunches and coffee, so from time to time we would meet at 5:00 a.m. and go to estate sales. We would be first in line and get all the great buys because she was great at spotting a bargain. This was a way to furnish our homes with beautiful antiques. We had a lot in common in that we were both business owners who were deeply in debt, our husbands both worked long hours, and we aspired to be the best parents we could for our children.

I always thought it would be fun to work with Joni, because she had great energy and empowered people to follow their dreams. She was just so much fun to be with. So one day when I was hired to do hair for an entire bridal party, I asked Joni if she would like come with me to help and have some fun. I figured she could hand me the pins, spray, and makeup, and other equipment while I worked my magic, and we would have a great day together. On the way, Joni told me about a network marketing meeting she had attended with her husband the night before. I was shocked and immediately told her that I was not interested and didn't want to hear anything about it. My experience with network marketers had been very negative, and the thought that Joni was actually considering it was astounding. People had approached me from time to time, and it seemed to me that they were always pushy and a bit sneaky. They never said outright that they were inviting me to a product presentation; rather they were inviting me for coffee or to visit with them at their home. One time a client invited me to her house, and when I turned up it was an Amway demonstration. I felt tricked, and from that point forward I wanted nothing to do with network marketers. There was no way I could ever see myself inviting someone to something and not tell them what they were coming to see. At one point, I overheard two clients in the salon arguing over who would recruit me, and neither one of them had ever discussed it with me. It was terrible and painfully obvious that they were only interested in what I could do for them—nothing to do with what I wanted. It was experiences like these that stopped me from ever looking into the real business of network marketing. As far as I was concerned, the whole thing was sneaky and underhanded, so hearing my friend Joni say she was interested blew my mind.

Regardless of me shutting her down in the car, she kept trying all day to get me to say yes, and eventually she said that if nothing else, I had to listen to her tape on the drive home. We always said it would be fun to do a business together, but network marketing was not what I had in mind. Finally I gave in and agreed to listen to the tape. Joni is a great closer, and I should have known that once I agreed to listen to the tape I was on a slippery slope. (Little did I know that we would both become wildly successful.) Sure enough, while we were listening to the tape she said that there was a meeting on Tuesday night, and for no other reason other than the fact that she was my close friend, I agreed to go.

I walked into that meeting room knowing in my heart of hearts that this whole evening was going to be a waste of time; however, I had promised Joni I would go with her, and that was that. All I can say is that I was not prepared for what happened as I watched the people around me and listened to the speakers. I don't know what I was expecting to see, but I was surrounded by happy, excited people who looked and talked just like me — not a sleazy salesperson in sight. Even the speakers looked like normal, everyday people, but they smiled when they spoke and they were excited about life and the future. They were enthusiastic and energized, and I was in awe of their love for life and what they were doing. The speakers that night lit a small fire of hope in me, and I started to dream little dreams. I turned to Joni and thanked her, saying, "I can do this!" And I really believed I could. It is hard to explain how elated I felt as I left that meeting. I believed that I was chained to that financial stress wheel forever, regardless of how hard I worked, and now I could see that there was a way to break those chains. All I had to do was work hard, and I knew how to do that. I understood the business right away, because I had been naturally networking and helping people ever since I became a hair stylist; it is just that no one ever sent me a check for my recommendations.

Joni and I energized each other and jumped into network marketing together that night, and before we left our first local meeting, I committed us to going to the next major event. We immediately started recruiting, and we made fun out of it like playing tag. When one of us recruited a new team member, we would call the other one and literally scream into the phone. Then it was up to the other to recruit someone and call back screaming. Our enthusiasm was infectious; everyone wanted to be in on the fun, and we both built excited teams in a very short period of time. It was wonderful, goofy, fun energy, and the dreaming took hold.

I started dreaming about working with energized, positive people like Joni every day. I wanted the fun and freedom. I loved my clientele for the most part, but I still had to be there in the salon. I couldn't go on a trip or take the kids somewhere on a Saturday simply because it was a beautiful day outside. June was wedding month, and my family life was put on hold. I put my clients ahead of my family because I thought I had to pay the bills, and also it must have been a self-esteem thing for me. My clients fed my self-esteem, and I wouldn't let them down no matter what, even at the expense of things my kids were doing. I didn't know I was doing it at the time. Network marketing gave me the hope that one day I would be free and able to give my family and me a better life.

Our first dream was to retire our husbands. Joni's husband worked in a mill, and Virgil was driving trucks. They were both tired and miserable, and we just knew we had to set them free as well as provide more for our children. Over the years, I have learned that dreams do come true, and they are the guiding lights toward a wonderful life.

Joni and I were new to this, but we knew that a big part of doing well was to hit the ground running and learn as fast as we could. Joni had found a collection of Big Al sales books at a garage sale, and we tore through them. They were funny, easy to read, and easy to understand. We handed them out among our team, and within our first month we organized a team trip to Edmonton, Canada, to hear Big Al speak. We took five girls with us and shared one room. You can imagine how little sleep we got and how much fun we had. Big Al has a unique sense of humor and is a great trainer. He is amazingly skilled at teaching the art of saying the right things to your prospect. Everything he taught made so much sense, and it was easy to understand, so we immediately implemented what we learned and it worked. Joni and I were in the people business before we took up network marketing, so we understood that people needed to be empowered in their lives, and Big Al's verbiage opened the gates for us to be able to help them.

We started traveling to events together, and regardless of our financial situation we always went to the two main company events each year. I am a great advocate of attending the big company events, because it reenergizes you and you get to meet and learn from other people running the same race as you. Events are not optional.

Against all odds, Joni and I started hanging out with top achievers of the company and we started going to their team events. Ultimately, both Joni and I thought that we could do this better than they did it, but at the start we knew we couldn't do it alone. We thought we had to have them to validate our opportunity and us, and this was probably true. We didn't have the big checks to prove that we were good, yet we did have people using the product. We also had to learn the whole process, because it's so much more than selling a product. It's more about helping people dream and helping them grow personally in their lives, which is what Joni and I have always been about.

I found that everything I learned in network marketing also helped me to better understand my hair salon clientele. I had a hunger to improve and grow in life. I started using phrases I had learned from Big Al in my salon. I would ask my clients questions and listen to what they wanted, and then, using Big Al verbiage, I would ask, "*Would it be OK if* I told you what I would do if I had carte blanche?" I would ask a client, "*Would it be OK if* I did such and such,*" or I would say, "I understand what you want; so with what I know *would it be OK if* I tell you what I would do if I had carte blanche, considering your face shape, hair, and so on." I practiced Big Al's verbiage in my salon every day and realized those five Big Al words—*would it be OK if*—were magic.

The excitement of going to company events and meeting incredibly motivated and successful people was unbelievable. Quite often, Joni and I shared rooms so that we could afford to make the trip. It was crowded and noisy, but it was fun, and the atmosphere was electric. We all wanted to grow personally and financially, and we were committed to doing whatever it took. All through my life, I had always felt like the odd one out, and now I felt like I had a home. I was like a sponge, absorbing everything around me. I read all the books, asked questions of my upline and the top money earners, and did everything and anything they asked of me.

Over the years, I have met many hardworking, successful network marketers, and in some instances I have been fortunate enough to become great friends with them and benefited from their mentoring and interest in my growth. I learned that network marketing is truly a sharing and caring environment; you just have to be committed and ask questions. The man who taught me the most in my early years and became an amazing mentor to me was Coby Gibson. Not since Gene Herrera, twenty-seven years earlier, had I come across someone who truly believed in me and could see my passion and hunger to make something of my life.

Coby was very poor when he started network marketing, but he had such a kind and sincere way about him that people looked past this and just wanted to work with him. Deep down, he was so driven that nobody could have told him no. He built a very successful business within nine months, and I was very impressed and wanted to know how he did it. I was still very new in my first company when I saw him onstage at a company event. I was immediately in awe of him. I later found out that his team loved him so much they had bought him the suit and tie so he could speak on stage, because he didn't have anything to wear to the event. I turned to Joni and said that we were going to meet him and his team tonight and get to know them. Joni looked at me as if to say, "You are one crazy woman—how are you going to do that?"

I watched where he walked from the stage after his heartfelt presentation.

He sat down at one of the top achievers' tables, and while my adrenalin was pumping, I jumped up and walked over to his table, kneeled down because awards were still going on, and said, "I'm Shauna, and it is so nice to meet you. I am so amazed at your story; it touched me. My group and I would like to meet with you and your group tonight. Is that possible? We want to know how you did this, because you were so inspiring." I think I said all of this without taking a breath. The first thing Coby said was, "I'm married." He's kind of goofy with a great sense of humor, and I said, "Well, so am I. Been married for twenty-seven years." I thought he was serious, and then he smiled and we both laughed. He agreed to meet with us later in the evening.

We ended up talking and laughing until three o'clock in the morning. There were four of us and four of his team. We sat at their feet and asked hundreds of questions. That's how Joni and I built our business—by asking, "How did you do this?" "Well, what did you say?" "And when they told you no, what did you do?"

We learned a lot and had so much fun together that we started hanging around with Coby's team at our major company events because they always had fun, and that's what we wanted too.

The greatest advice Coby gave to us that first night was how to handle rejection:

Well, it's like if you offer someone a cup of coffee, and they say no thanks, you don't run off and start crying or feel sad and rejected; you go to the next person and offer a cup of coffee. Later on, that first person might want coffee, but just not now.

This advice has stayed with me forever, and to this day, when someone says no, I immediately think, "Maybe later they will want to have a cup of coffee."

Joni and I would get inspired every time we were around him. Once he came down to Seattle to attend a personal growth seminar, and we offered to pick him up at the airport and take him wherever he needed to go. We picked him up and took him to all of his appointments, and in the evening we took him out to our favorite restaurant by the airport and spent the evening talking to him. Joni and I made up a song for Coby to one of our favorite country songs. The song was all about how much Coby had inspired us, and I remember like it was yesterday, we sang the song to him outside the restaurant standing in the rain; he was so touched that he cried.

Unfortunately, not all the advice I received from top achievers worked out as well as Coby's. I had only been in the industry four months when a top achiever who was all about volume advised me to take two months off and just work the business. He said the quickest way to grow my business was to show people how I quit my day job and developed walkaway income. With my naïveté, I believed him, because I could see with my own eyes people in the company who were full time and looked to be doing very well. He said, "Just take a leave of absence; your business will grow so fast that even you won't believe it, and people will want to know what you are doing." I took him at his word and canceled all my appointments, closing my home salon for two months. I believed in network marketing, and I thought he knew what he was talking about because he looked successful and I was a newbie drowning in debt. My mind-set was that I am a fast learner and I know how to work hard, so I went for it.

During those two months, I had no regular income, and at the same time I was borrowing money to go to the events and buying the recommended personal development books. I was not just investing in the books for myself but buying extra books for my team members and giving them to them for free in an attempt to make sure they were following through like I was. I was so blinded by the lifestyle this top achiever had portrayed that I started investing more money than the average person would, because I was so hungry to make it happen. Sadly, at the end of the two months, all I had was a stack of bills and a frustrated and confused clientele, some of whom had moved on to other hair stylists. Furthermore, my networking business was full of people I had recruited out of desperation. People know when they are being recruited by a desperate person, and it is hard because they are turned off by the sense of need on my behalf rather than theirs. They must have felt like I did when people were trying to recruit me for their own benefit, and here I was doing the exact same thing. On the other hand, I discovered later in life that recruiting is easy when you have a heartfelt belief that this is the best thing for them, and you can only know that when you have taken the time to get to know them.

I was too naïve and new to network marketing to make it happen that quickly, but I didn't know that at the time. I reopened my home salon and worked hard to make up for lost time, with two months of debt and a group of people I had managed to either confuse or alienate.

I have to give my husband credit for putting up with it all. He saw that I really believed in the business, and he believed that I could retire him. He saw the dream, and even though networking was not something he was personally comfortable with, he stood by me during the difficult early years. I learned an incredible lesson that winter: don't jump ship until you have a life raft handy. Another wonderful mentor, Stan Barker, recommends that you should have about eighteen months' wages in the bank before you jump ship, and that's great advice. Every day was another opportunity to learn another lesson.

Joni and I had been working our way up the ladder at our first network marketing company and having a lot of fun in the process, even though we were spending more money than we were making. It was a little like two steps forward and one step back. We made every mistake under the sun, and in spite of it, we managed to progressively build our teams and stay motivated and happy.

Originally, I had been inspired to join network marketing because it looked like a great place to meet exciting, positive, successful people and to learn how to become one of them. Unfortunately, I got too close to the fire in my first company, and the last couple of years there were very rough. The gloss had worn off, and I was in deep with the business and financially. I experienced firsthand the lying and manipulation that went on among my upline and peers, and after many months of soul-searching, I decided to leave. It was a heart wrenching time, because I had fully invested in the company and my closest friends were all involved. It took me months of agony and sleepless nights, because for me it was like leaving my family, but I couldn't work any longer in an environment that I found so unethical, and I couldn't promote an opportunity that I no longer believed in.

It was Coby who introduced me to my second company. It was a wise move on my behalf to follow Coby and his advice, because I believe that if I had stayed at the first company, I might have quit network marketing altogether—the existing culture had become one of "every man for himself."

I left the first company disillusioned, embarrassed, and heartbroken. I jumped right into the second company, rolled up my sleeves, and went to work. It represented a tax-related product that helped people minimize their taxes and had a tax-auditing component. There was a new excitement and an energy that came from a company that was on a roll and created value for people. Industry leaders were making enormous incomes, and I saw and felt what it was like to be in momentum for the first time. This tax company was already experiencing momentum when I heard about it, and I started making money immediately. It was fun and very easy to sell, because everyone wants to save money on their taxes. I used to play the product video while I was working in my salon, and my clients couldn't help but listen. They would ask questions about it and want to try it out. I didn't have to do anything except show the video and the product sold itself. Sounds a little too good to be true, doesn't it?

Unfortunately a government regulatory department closed the company down within six months and I was left stranded and embarrassed again. I had invested several years in my first company, and now after only six months in the second company I was devastated and would soon be looking for another company. It was at this time that I began to question myself and my abilities in network marketing. It was then that Coby introduced me to my next extraordinary mentor, Stan Barker, and with his guidance and encouragement, I decided not to quit.

Stan is a loveable, fatherly kind of guy, and he helped heal my broken "network marketing heart." He was like an elder statesman for network marketing. Stan already had a successful network marketing career under his belt with Amway, and he had worked with the big boys like Bill Britt and Dexter Yeager. Compared to these men, the top achievers I had met so far were juniors.

Stan was then, and still is, a relationship guy. He would quickly and easily make you feel warm and comfortable talking to him. His passion was personal growth, and one of his favorite sayings was, "You'll see it when you believe it."

He was personal friends with Bill Britt and Jim Brooks, who were also proponents of personal growth. I had first noticed the importance of personal growth at my first network marketing company, and I quickly learned that you have to grow yourself or you're never going to attract the right people and grow your business.

Stan believed in me and took me under his wing, and for that I am forever grateful. He had enormous faith and helped me to believe that there were great networking companies out there with experienced senior people who were interested in helping newer people succeed in the business. He taught me about the importance of the meeting after the meeting and storytelling. His personal stories were inspiring. I will always remember one story in particular that Stan told. Bill Britt threw Stan the keys to his new Lamborghini and told him to take it for a spin for one week. It was Stan who kept us going after the tax company folded. He said, "OK, we don't have a company, but we have each other," so we continued to have our weekly meetings for the next two months. He rented a place and we trained using old Amway tapes. We kept learning, and I learned how important that was. We'd go to Johnny's restaurant in Puyallup and talk, make friends, and learn from each other. We supported and inspired one another, saying things like, "I'm still here you're still here. We don't know where it's going to go, but we have hope." Stan kept our networking family together and our spirits up as we searched for a new home. He is still an enormous, inspiring force, and he is now into his late seventies. Our group ended up going separate ways into different opportunities, but we have always stayed in touch and remain friends to this day.

A few years into my network marketing adventure, I decided to open a hair salon in downtown Enumclaw. My home salon was growing, and parking was becoming a problem now that my youngest son was driving.

An office space in an old building became available in downtown Enumclaw, and I decided to move my salon out of the house and into this wonderful space. What a freeing and exciting time that was. The rent was so reasonable, I just couldn't refuse. Opening the Red Door Salon was definitely a major event in my life, and my daughter Heidi, who was a decorative artist, came home from New Orleans to help with the renovations. It was her idea to paint the salon door red and call it the Red Door Salon. But it wasn't until much later, when I stepped through that door for the very last time, that I realized its true significance in my life.

Nathan is my third child, and he was a teenager when I opened the Red

Door Salon. He would come to the salon on Wednesday nights as I was growing my networking business and help with my team calls. I would write out a little script and give him a list of people to call, because I was doing hair. He was terrific. He would call them and tell them, "My mom told me to call and ask you to get on this call tonight." I developed my business through weekly team calls, which I would conduct while doing hair. My clients loved it, and quite often they would end up asking for information about the business opportunities. Money was starting to be less of a problem, and I was able to retire my old rust bucket car for a newer model. The feeling of being able to buy a newer car was incredible. I didn't pay cash, but the monthly payments weren't hard to make.

Soon, I came across a start-up company with a nutritional antioxidant product. I was innocent enough to think because it was a start-up company it was a really good opportunity for me to get to the top quickly, and I particularly liked their trainer. There were a few credible networkers already involved, so I joined up.

I wasn't that into the product, because it was not a visual and an emotional product, which was very important to me.

Since then I have learned that a start-up is not always the best company to join. You have to be really careful of start-up companies. Statistics show that until a company is into its fifth year, it is not really stable, and you are going to go through ups and downs. Most start-ups don't make it.

The last few years had been pretty stressful. I had joined three companies over the past six years in an attempt to find the right fit for me, and so far all I had to show for my commitment and hard work was a pile of debt bigger than I had started with. I felt that I had officially became a member of the "NFL" (No Friends Left) club. The interesting thing is that I never considered quitting network marketing, because I believed in the profession and I was convinced that if I could find the right company my future would take off. Thank you, Stan Barker! Even though I was having a rough time, I learned many valuable lessons from each company and met some great, inspiring people. The first company taught me that ethics and values are more important to me than any check. The second company taught me to personally meet the company owners and if it looks too good to be true, then it just might be. The greatest thing I learned from my third company was the importance to me of a product being visual and emotional. It was obvious that I could only work with a product that I would use even if I didn't work for the company, because I had to have a personal story to tell. So far I had learned that I needed to believe in the company owners, the product, and me. I had come to know by then that I already had an unshakable belief in the profession of network marketing.

The other benefit from the past six years was harder for anyone to see except me, and that was knowing that even though I was still chained to debt and locked inside four walls, I was getting closer to breaking free and reaching my dreams. I had passion, hunger, and belief that wouldn't quit—nor would I.

I would like to say that the fourth company was the one, but unfortunately, it was just another six-month wonder. This was where I first met Carol Taylor. She was one of the top leaders, and there was something about her that made me want to work with her. She exuded integrity, and it was Carol who attracted me to the fourth company. This company distributed a nutritional product range, and it had been around for twenty years, so it looked solid. However, I can honestly say that apart from meeting Carol, it didn't excite me that much. Even though I had joined and I was personally taking and selling the product, I was only halfheartedly involved. After the last few companies, I had decided to take it slowly and see how I felt before I started spreading the news.

I attended two big events, and it was at the second event that the company launched their weight-loss product. Earlier in 2001, Virgil and I had divorced after thirty-one years of marriage, and I had gained weight due to the stress and associated depression. Obviously, the start of this new century was not going so well for me. I thought that a weight-loss product would be a good bet, because if it worked I would have a great personal story to tell everyone. My idea was good and I was committed, but unfortunately the weight didn't come off as fast as promised and I only lost about five pounds, which was not so exciting. Meanwhile, Carol Taylor and her crew had moved to a new company they had been testing out, and as soon as I heard this I followed suit.

I was truly in search of a home. I desperately wanted to feel that exciting family feeling I had felt initially in the first company, and as soon as I met the owners of my fifth company I knew that I had found my home at last. I had been wandering the networking wasteland for seven years, and finally my persistence paid off. I found a company that had everything I was looking for, and I am just as happy and excited today as I was back in 2002.

Finally, within a year of joining my current company, all my hard work and persistence started to pay off. I continued to work diligently in my salon, but now I had a secondary income that was growing. I was earning more money than I was spending. The products offered by this company are visual and emotional, and I had a personal result that people could see. I decided not to tell everyone about my new company until I was completely satisfied that the products did what the company said they would.

I started the program and allowed my results to speak for themselves. It was not long before my hairstyling clients noticed my shrinking silhouette and started asking me what I was doing to get such great changes in my body and skin. This was such a turnaround: I actually had people asking me for information and I could tell them my story of transformation with genuine enthusiasm and excitement. I am a baby boomer, and excess weight, aging, and funding my old age were issues that constantly weighed on my mind. Now I had joined a company that solved all three of these problems. The products promote healthy weight management and also include a supplement that combats the aging process. We all want this powerful combination, so expanding my network marketing business has been easy since the day I started with them. The products provide me with the platform to make a lot of money and stay young enough to enjoy it.

There are hundreds of different network marketing companies, and some of them are really good, allowing you to make money. The issue for you to work out is what type of products or services resonate best with you. You have to love and believe in the company and its products and services, and you genuinely need to know that you are helping people through this company. I sincerely love my company and what it stands for, so it is easy to sell, and in return it is keeping me youthful and financially fit and healthy.

My approach to joining this company was very different from the previous four, in that not only had I learned some valuable lessons but I applied those lessons. I believe in the company owners. I went to the first event within the first month, and I got to look them in the eye and personally question them about the company and its products. I asked myself if I really believed them, and I did. I think this is something you should do. Go to the company HQ. If there is not an event coming up, you should fly in, meet the owners, meet the people, look at everything, and kick the tires. This is a long-term home and family for you. Don't just jump in on someone else's say so like I did many years ago, and don't get swept up in the hype of a new company launch. Do yourself and your family a big favor and check it out thoroughly. You could lose a lot more than your credibility. You could lose your dreams and hope. I sailed close to the wind a couple of times and could have just as easily walked away from network marketing if not for my belief that it was my path to freedom.

After I knew with all my heart that I had found the right company, I went back to the people I loved the most, because I did not want to leave them behind. I remember going over to Starbuck's one morning and calling my friend Joni. We hadn't worked together for a few years, and I knew the other companies I had worked my way through were not for her, but this company was perfect for her. I knew it in my heart. I begged her for an hour just to give me her social, and she said no. At one stage I felt like saying, "Are we friends or not? I'm doing you an enormous favor." She kept saying no. That was a good lesson for me. I just had to wait until her timing was right.

Heartfelt Network Marketing is about relationships and caring and understanding what the other person needs and wants. Just because you are close friends with someone doesn't mean you always know what they need or want. I had presumed that I knew my friend Joni very well, so when I called her up after a long absence I heard myself saying, "I love you, I've missed you, and I do not want you to do this the hard way like I've been doing. I know where you've been, I know where you are, and I know what's going to happen with that, and I have a fantastic way out for you." What she heard me say was, "Have I got a deal for you."

It took her two years to come around, but when she finally did, she surpassed me within two years. I was so excited and cheered her on as she started and built an incredible leg that now consists of eight millionaires. Sometimes it feels good when you are proven right.

Growing your business and being able to build a wonderful life for your family is the greatest gift. My youngest son Nathan was taking acting classes, and there was a special acting school audition going on in New York that he wanted to go to. He was fifteen at the time, and acting was everything to him. I had never been to New York, so I decided that we would go together. The wonderful memories of exploring New York together far exceeded the ten thousand dollars it cost. I was still in the Red Door Salon, but we had a solid secondary income stream now, which made it all possible. I could pay for the trip and close the salon for a week and still have money coming in. A few years before, I couldn't have done it. I did notice, though, that as my network marketing business grew, my time in the salon started decreasing.

A book that really changed me was *The E-Myth*, by Michael Gerber. In the book, Gerber explains that as a business owner you are the CEO and manager of your own business. He then goes on to list all the other roles and responsibilities of a business owner. I hated being the CEO and I never wanted to be the manager or the sales coordinator. I just wanted to be the technician and artist. Yet here I was with my own salon. I hated all of it except the interaction with people and my craft. It was while reading Gerber's book that a light bulb went on in my head and I realized that I didn't actually want to own a salon. I wanted to become a professional network marketer and fly. The only thing that had changed since school, when I sat in class dreaming about being free to run and explore, was the number of hours until recess. I still longed to break out of my cell and the mountains of debt that went with it. Becoming a full-time professional network marketer was my key to freedom, and I was going to take it.

In 2006, I closed the Red Door Salon forever and became a professional Heartfelt Network Marketer.

Stan Barker had always said that you have to have at least a year and a half of your old wage in the bank before you leave your day job. This way you are not recruiting out of desperation. I don't remember exactly where I was financially when I quit, but it had gotten to the point where I was traveling quite a lot and constantly changing people's hair appointments. Doing hair was no longer fun, and it was embarrassing having to change client appointments all the time. There was also all this residual income coming in.

In 2002, I earned $19,000, then $59,000, followed by $89,000, and then finally six figures in 2005 when I made $129,000. It took me ten years overall to get to the six-figure mark, but once I found my niche my yearly income began to grow at a much faster rate.

I hadn't really planned an exit strategy because I had my head down, taking care of both businesses and handling the never-ending day to day issues.

When Virgil and I divorced, my youngest son and I had moved into a three-room office suite behind the Red Door and turned it into our home. I continued to work twelve-hour days, and a new feature of my life as a hair stylist was a morning visit to my chiropractor. My body had started paying the price of years of bending over clients and wash basins. My networking income was on the rise and had surpassed my hair salon revenue, and when I coupled this with my deteriorating back problem, I readily made the life-changing decision to close the Red Door Salon and step into the sunshine forever.

My clients were devastated to hear the news, and my decision did not come a minute too soon. On the very last day that I worked in the Red Door Salon, my back gave out completely during my last hair appointment. My client had to push her chair—and me—up against the wall so I could stay upright to finish her hair, and I can still remember the pain. While I was jammed between the salon wall and the chair, my client asked what I was going to do and why I would close down such a great little salon. She told me that nobody wanted me to quit my day job and they didn't believe I could make it in network marketing. I was a little shocked, so I told her how much money I was making and explained the financial side of things and a little about the side benefits of being a professional network marketer. She instantly asked why I hadn't told her sooner and signed up there and then.

As soon as I locked the door for the last time and stepped into the sunshine, I knew I had made the right decision to close the Red Door Salon and escape the four walls I had been trying to escape since my school days. I could now enjoy life and walk in the park in the middle of the day or go up into the mountains to ski or join my kids at a street fair. My hairstyling career hadn't been torture—it was fun, and for the most part I enjoyed the time with my clients—but it was so structured. My time was never my own. I was always at the beck and call of my clients, regardless of my personal life. One of the times I realized I had been set free was when my son and I went on a road trip for three weeks. We took that much time off because I was making money by then and it was possible to go on a little road trip up to Montana and meet some people and see my brother and my mom. We had a Honda Element that we could make into a camper, and it was so much fun. We didn't even have a plan. We visited my brother in Colorado, drove through Yellowstone, and just did things we wanted to do.

It has been several years since that day, and I have achieved dreams far beyond wanting to have a store-bought dress or drive a new car. I have traveled the world and continue to help thousands of people realize their dreams. Every day is a great day in my world. I get to mix with positive, excited people and spread hope everywhere I go.

Every time I meet a new person, I am reminded of the epiphany I experienced that first night I went to a network marketing meeting:

I was in a room filled with people who looked no better than me, but they were excited about life and going for their dreams. Seeing them made me realize that I could do it too.

There was also the equally powerful second epiphany that came a few weeks later at the company meeting, when I heard a speaker say:

Make your strengths productive and your weaknesses irrelevant.

Sometimes just a few words can change someone's life. I found a way to get off the financial stress wheel and give my family and me a future with options.

I was not an overnight success, but I was empowered by hope and my dreams. I studied the industry, focused on learning all I could about personal development, and worked diligently. At the start, it was difficult because I didn't know what I was doing. I just did what the top achievers told me to do. It never felt quite right, but I was a newbie, so I figured it was just me. Five companies and fifteen years later, I can tell you that my gut feeling was right. I eventually stopped listening to everyone and started to listen to myself. As soon as I did this, my network marketing career changed for the better. With every little success I became more confident in my different approach to network marketing, and I ultimately developed my Heartfelt Network Marketing Manifesto. I have always come from the position of genuinely wanting to help people feel better about themselves and give them hope for the future.

I found that network marketing was a very doable thing; building my network marketing business on a part-time basis while still running my salon gave me hope, and with hope I kept dreaming.

The principals of Heartfelt Network Marketing have allowed me to dramatically change my life physically and financially, my family's life, and the lives of tens of thousands of people across the country.

I sold my shop in 2006 because my passion for making a difference in people's lives and providing them with a space where they felt understood and heard had taken a different turn. I always believed that I was making a difference in people's lives, but I was very aware that it was only for a short time—maybe it would last six to eight weeks until their next hair appointment. I wanted to focus on helping people make *lifetime* changes. I am talking about a legacy that will affect future generations.

It isn't complicated. Most people are drowning in despair and hopelessness due to their never-ending problem of continually running out of time and money. This alone can kill you with stress and the effect it has on your heart health. They go through each day feeling that there is nothing they can do to change their future; all hope has gone and their dreams have turned to dust, so they don't even try. I have come across this scenario time and time again. My role is to listen and understand what is going on in a person's life. If it is appropriate, I will respectfully ask permission to tell them my personal story. Often just knowing that I don't have a college degree and that I really did start out in life on the wrong side of the tracks gives them hope that maybe, just maybe, they too can break free of their daily depression.

Had I not gone against the norm when I was a young girl, I'm sure that I would have never discovered my current career. This incredible career has changed the lives of my children, my grandchildren, and tens of thousands of people that I have been able to touch both directly and indirectly because of my story and by sharing what I consider a gift of Heartfelt Network Marketing.

I am a Heartfelt Network Marketer, and I am proud of it. Why wouldn't I be? It is an honorable profession that affords me the time and money to help people physically and emotionally. It is through this industry that I was able to save my eldest son's life when he nearly died from drug addiction. I had the money to keep him in rehab for as long as he needed to fully recover, and today I am proud to say that he has joined the family business. I have been able to buy my mother a home that she loves and be generous with my resources. Money doesn't change who you are; it allows you to be more of who you are.

It is time the stigma is lifted from network marketing and people are given a chance to explore the opportunities without prejudice. My goal is to raise the bar of the industry and, in doing so, help the tens of thousands of single parents and families struggling through life to see that there are options. There are alternatives to lack of time, money, and fun. This industry has a great deal to offer—not least is the opportunity to meet and mix with people who are focused on personal growth and realizing their dreams. Even if it does takes years and there are challenges to overcome, the point is they are doing something about it and growing.

I know what it is like to be on the outside looking in. I used to want to fit in so badly that I would go on shopping sprees and buy stylish clothes so that we looked like everyone else, all the time knowing that we didn't have the money to pay the credit card bills at the end of the month. I used to be so scared about the bills that I would hide the unopened envelopes in a box, hoping they would magically disappear. Thanks to the personal development training and the great speakers and top achievers I have met in the network marketing industry, I learned that I didn't need to change to fit in; I just needed to find a group of friends and colleagues who were like me. The network marketing industry is overflowing with caring, hardworking, motivated, fun, supportive individuals who started with nothing and then found hope and started to dream. I am one of them, and I am proof that it can be done without compromising your ethics and alienating your family and friends—though I did in the beginning. Mixing with like-minded people takes all the stress out of being you.

I don't resent starting out with two strikes against me, because it gave me the chance to learn a very important lesson:

If it is to be, it is up to me.

For those of you who are concerned that I have focused on money a little too much, please understand that money is a source of energy. Money allows you to be free and to help others:

You can't feed the poor when you are one of them.

My wonderful husband Dr. Scott Peterson has encouraged me to spread my story and the gift of Heartfelt Network Marketing to as many people as humanly and technologically possible. Everyone deserves to have options in life and a chance to reclaim their hopes and dreams. I want you to know what it is like to feel free—to be able to help your elderly parents, pay for your children's college education, or contribute to a cause you are passionate about.

Now you know my story. I hope you can see how doable network marketing is as long as you believe in what you are doing and have a burning desire in the pit of your stomach to make a difference in your life and that of your family.

I am passionate about helping people. I don't have a traditional college degree, but I believe that I've earned a PhD in life and now it is my turn to pay it forward.

Will you be the one to make a difference in your family?

1955 - Rigby, Idaho, Shauna as a serious 2 year old.

1961 - Salt Lake City, Utah (Swede Town). (From L to R) sister Sharon (10 years), Shauna (8 years), brother Dean (5 years), brother Denny (2 years). The family when we first moved to Salt Lake City. This was an exciting time because it is where I met Jill and we discovered the enchanting "Swede Town". I was very maternal at this time: Denny and Dean were "My babies". We attended a one room school-house here.

1956 - Rigby, Idaho (From L to R) Shauna and sister Sharon. Mother was an excellent streamstress. She made all of our clothes and sewed a doll dress to match!

1969 - Salt Lake City, Utah. Shauna (Sweet 16) started Darrell's College of Beauty (Cosmetology School) in Salt Lake. She was living in Swede Town at the time.

Shauna, stylist and owner of the original Red Door Salon in Enumclaw, Washington.

1955 - Shauna at age 2 (one the left) with her mother, father and sister.

1961 - Salt Lake City, Utah (Swede Town). Shauna's parents paid $6000 for this house in Swede Town. They paid $55 a month until it was paid off. This was right across the street from Grandma's house: two bedrooms and one bath: four kids in one bedroom! Shaun lived here from the summer before second grade 'til the summer of 7th grade. We then moved to Bountiful, Utah for 2 years.

1961 - Salt Lake City, Utah (Swede Town). Grandma's house, my Mom's "Family Home" after they left the log cabin at Dusceme, Utah. Grandmas kitchen was always open and we had many family gatherings there. It was just one block away from the railroad tracks, where the bums lived and came to Grandmas for handout. In 1961 my parents bought the house across the street.

1980's - Brothers, sisters and cousins with Shauna (in the middle).

Shauna's three children.

The Ekstrom family with Shauna, husband and mother.

Recent photos - Shauna with her sons.

Shauna with her daughter, Heidi.

Shauna with her daughter, Heidi, and grandkids.

2012 - Shauna at the Del Coronado. Hotel for the "Top Achievers Event" in San Diego. She was one of the Top Achievers that year.

Shauna with Jimmy Smith.

Atlantis, Bahamas - Peter Oelmann, Shauna, Carole Taylot & Scott.

Shauna and husband, Dr. Scott Peterson.

Section II

The Dawn of Heartfelt Network Marketing

Heartfelt Network Marketing is all about sharing and helping people. It is not the hard-sell or even the soft-sell method—it is the nonsell method.

The Principles of Heartfelt Marketing

Heartfelt Network Marketing (HNM) is the culmination of the life lessons I have learned over the past sixty-plus years and my passion for helping people to see that there is hope and that you can dream.

Learn from the Experiences of Others

I am living my dream today because I discovered network marketing and, believing that it was my way out, took it with both hands. My only regret is that I cared too much what well-meaning broke people thought about making money and status. I think it was because of my lack of education that I doubted myself and cared so much about what others thought, instead of making up my own mind about network marketing.

I was forty-four years old before I had the courage to go for it. By then, my children were twenty-five, twenty-two, and eight years old. I often wonder how different parenthood would have been had I had the time and the freedom I have now. You, on the other hand, have the opportunity to leapfrog a great many of my mistakes and get straight to the good stuff.

My daughter Heidi is a great example of someone who has taken full advantage of learning from my mistakes.

Heidi left home at eighteen and moved to New Orleans. She worked for a couple of years and then put herself through university, ending up with a degree in fine arts from UNO. She excelled in fine art and eventually married and started a family. Heidi had listened to my struggles and excitement throughout my early years of network marketing and had come to the conclusion that I was simply crazy— she never saw the rabbit I was chasing. She wanted nothing to do with network marketing, even though I had registered her and her brothers and tried on several occasions to explain the benefits of joining the family firm.

It wasn't until she was going through the same problems most mothers go through, trying to juggle their time between a career and a young family, that she decided to look into Heartfelt Network Marketing. By this time, I had calmed down and it had become a part of my very being.

I discovered network marketing after my two eldest children had become young adults and were living their own lives. I experienced a long, arduous journey of trial and error, divorce, family stress, and ongoing financial worries while learning how to network market on my terms.

Heidi, on the other hand, was able to take the shortcut and go straight to the Heartfelt Network Marketing way. Her girls are still in elementary school and are benefiting from a full-time mom and the financial resources network marketing is providing them. Heidi started making serious money within months of starting her network marketing career.

Heidi was able to transition quickly because she could see firsthand what she needed to do, and she did it. She had the benefit of knowing the right way to go about building her business through relationships, caring, and sharing her story—she followed the Heartfelt Network Marketing way.

Heidi, at forty-two, has it all, whereas at forty-two I still had yet to see the light.

She works approximately four hours a day, four days a week. She has time to be a hands-on mom, running her three little girls around to their six different after school hobbies, going on vacations with her husband and the girls, and taking on the role of general contractor, managing the construction of their wonderful new home.

Heidi now earns a serious multiple figure annual income, and I am a very proud mom.

As far as her passion for art and all things artistic, Heidi now has the time to pursue her career as a true artist, uncompromising and guilt-free. Heidi's life is so different from mine at the same age, and for this I am eternally grateful to our honorable profession.

The moral of the story is to get going now and learn from top achievers and others like myself who have learned the lessons and want to pay it forward. You don't have to take fifteen years to get where I am. I don't want you to waste another minute, because that is a minute you will never get back.

Here are the six basic building blocks to your network marketing career:

- What is your dream?
- Understand the network marketing industry.
- Appreciate your role as an honorable professional.
- Define your personal growth path.
- Remember three key beliefs—yourself, the product, the company.
- Build your business through fun, relationships, and storytelling.

If I can do it, you can too.

I often hear people say this, and I agree with them, provided we add a few conditions:

- You have to know what you want and why.
- You need the drive and hunger to go the distance.
- You must be passionate about your chosen path.

The only thing going for me for the first twenty years of my life was my hunger for freedom and the hope that there was more to life than working, worrying, tiredness, misery, and stress.

I was born into a working-class family where the lack of money was always a hot topic between my parents. I left high school at fifteen; at seventeen I married a lovely man who at times earned a dollar an hour, and I was pregnant with my first child at eighteen. You wouldn't be blamed for thinking that only in the movies could a girl with this start in life end up building a million-dollar business and have the time and financial freedom to help her family, friends, and complete strangers. My dear friend and graphic artist Bunker Hill Bradley says that my life has all the hallmarks of a great movie, but it isn't make believe. Every step, every lesson learned, every tear, every triumph, every mistake, every laugh is real. I dared to dream, and ultimately I found a way to make my dreams become my reality through helping others.

Network marketing is the path I chose, and my driving force over the years has been belief in myself and the absolute knowledge that network marketing is a way to have a life. It is the vehicle that allows true freedom to choose what I want to do with my life. I help others to dream, grow, and hope, and in doing so I get to live my dreams.

I am not being melodramatic or romantic. I am sincere and genuine when I say that following the Heartfelt Network Marketing caring and sharing philosophy was my path to an incredible life, and it can also help you along your path to whatever it is that you dream of.

Never give up or quit on your dreams.

Your Dream

Sometimes people have been living under the sheer weight of their everyday lives for so long that they have stopped dreaming. I know I had stopped dreaming for years before I found network marketing. Your Heartfelt Network Marketing career starts with your dream. What is it that you want out of life? Your dream gives you direction and motivation. It helps you to get over the hard times and inspires you to grow and extend yourself.

The Network Marketing Industry

Heartfelt Network Marketing is more about the human side of network marketing, so I have not dedicated too much time to explaining the ins and outs of the network marketing industry. There are already hundreds of great books that talk about network marketing in great depth, and I don't need to add to this list. However for those of you who are new to this industry, I have included a basic outline of network marketing and the prevailing myths that surround this incredible profession. This will give you a good foundation to work from while you are expanding your knowledge on the subject.

The Honorable Profession

I firmly believe that being a heartfelt network marketer is an honorable profession. We help people to believe in themselves, to hope, to dream, and to grow. We also help them to see options for their future and the future of their families. There are also many times when we have helped them find their path toward their dreams, and they have succeeded beyond their imagination.

We approach the business of network marketing from a position of caring about the other person, and from this position we can work out if our solution is a good fit for them. If so, then we both win. Our prospect starts their wonderful journey toward their dreams, and we move closer to ours.

Be more concerned with your character than with your reputation, for your character is what you are, while your reputation is merely what others think you are.

—Dale Carnegie

Personal Growth

Network marketing is a people business, starting with you. The entire industry is focused on personal development and growth. Sometimes I think I invest more time and money in growing myself as a person than the actual business. I believe that this is OK, because the more I grow, the more helpful I am to the people around me, and the faster my business grows.

The more you learn about subjects like goal setting, persistence, follow-through, time management, motivation, and body language, the more skilled you will be in your business and everyday life.

You are building your own network marketing business, and this takes time and skills that you may not have at the start, but with persistence and working in your network marketing environment, where you are surrounded by like-minded people, you will grow and so will your business.

The Three Key Beliefs—Yourself, Your Product, Your Company

Belief is a key factor in everything you do when it comes to building your network marketing business. Believing in yourself—your ability to grow, learn, be patient, stay focused, and apply yourself every day—is the most important attribute to becoming a successful heartfelt network marketer. You have no chance of growing yourself or your business if you don't believe you can. I devote an entire section of this book to self-belief to help you over this potential hurdle.

Believing in yourself is one thing, but a heartfelt network marketer is a genuine caring person, and that means you must believe in your product or service as well as the company itself.

The product or service must be one that you know delivers on its promise and you are proud to stand behind it.

The same goes for the company itself. You are helping people start their dream machines and build their own businesses, so you want to make sure to the best of your ability that the company will not let them down.

Even if a company does fail, so long as you maintain your relationships and team you will find another home and keep building.

Heartfelt Network Marketing Is About the Other Person

You already have your goals and dreams worked out, and you're on your path toward achieving them. When you meet a new person or a prospect, you are interested in his or her hopes and dreams. Try to step into the other person's shoes for a while so that you can understand his or her position and point of view. The more you understand what is important to this person's challenges and aspirations, the more equipped you will be to develop a great rapport and a relationship.

You want to uncover what your prospect dreams about—and if he or she doesn't dream anymore, you want to help him or her to get going again.

When you are telling your dream story, watch out for the telltale signs that your prospect is relating and wants to chime in. Ask nonthreatening questions about his or her aspirations and what he or she wanted to grow up to be as a child.

You care—give them hope—and dream with them.

Sometimes people have little or no self-esteem and dare not dream. It is your task to show them that they have good qualities and move them toward self-actualization. You will be surprised how well a person responds to even a little belief from another.

Inspire them to dream and hope by setting an example through your story. Try not to sound like you are bragging or showing off. Sometimes, through my story, I reveal how I was able to buy my mother a home, pay for months of drug rehab for my son, and pay for product for nearly six months for a friend to get back on track with her health. I then mention a couple of things like being able to sleep at night, taking my grandkids shopping at the Gap without once looking at the price tags, and other lighthearted, fun things.

Help the other person to create a positive visual of their future, the product, and the honorable profession of sharing.

Building Your Business through Fun, Relationships, and Storytelling

The fastest way to a miserable day is talking to anyone who comes within earshot about your product or business. How would you feel if someone you didn't know came rushing up to you, shook your hand, and started to tell you about this great opportunity?

Take it one step at a time. Take your time and get to know people. Build relationships with them. Sometimes it can take me three to four instances with someone new before I can honestly say we have the beginnings of a relationship.

The great thing about working for myself is that there is no one with a stopwatch and a procedure manual keeping tabs on me. I can go as slowly or as quickly as the situation requires.

You don't need to rush in and try to fill your first meeting with everyone you know. Think about it and, when possible, invite people you have already met. This will make it a lot easier on your guest speaker, your guests, and you. Go slowly so you can learn as you go and not burn all your prospects in one go. A small group of people who already like and trust you is far more important than a room full of strangers, otherwise known as cold prospects. Then again, why wouldn't you at least want to share this with those you love? Give them the option to say yes or no. Then, if the answer is no, ask if you can let them know how it's going in six months or a year.

Jimmy Smith's philosophy on the word no is great:

If they knew what I know, they wouldn't say no. So until I can share what I know and they can really hear it, no just means "later."

A long time ago, I learned a very valuable lesson from Stan Barker, and that is the importance of the meeting after the meeting. This is when the formalities are over and everyone is more relaxed. It is a great time to start to get to know the people around you and begin the relationship phase. It is the best time to find out what they want and maybe tell your story and get them to start dreaming. This is where the fun begins.

I slowly did what others advised against—I did not set out with an agenda. I felt that relating and listening to the other person first was more important than a sales agenda. Your meetings should always have an element of fun and not just be a one-sided information fest.

Heartfelt Network Marketing is a storytelling business.

Heartfelt Network Marketing is not sales. It is sharing relevant parts of your story and how you are traveling along your path toward your dreams. Your aim is to help people dream and to give them hope. If you feel that it is appropriate, introduce them to an additional choice in their lives, bearing in mind that it is up to *them* to make the choice.

Getting to know the other person is paramount if you are genuinely interested in helping them widen their horizons and expose them to options that they may never have considered until now.

I believe the best way to do this is to initiate the conversation by asking them a little about themselves. Even shy people will usually relax when they can talk about themselves.

A great opener to get your prospect to start talking is for you to ask what their current profession is. When they tell you, surprise them by complimenting them on their profession rather than putting it down. After all, this is their day job, and you should start by assuming they are having fun and enjoy it. If they are not, they will very quickly tell you, which is a great opening for you to introduce other options. This is a great tip I learned from Big Al.

Once you get them talking, actively listen to what they are saying and how they are saying it. Often it is *how* we tell a story that provides more clues than the story itself. Your objective is to determine if they have a need you can fulfill. If you feel that you can relate to their story, ask permission to tell them a brief version of your story.

Everyone loves stories, and the one thing you can be sure of is that you can tell your story from the heart. Telling your story helps open up the channels of communication. Storytelling is so important that I have dedicated a chapter of this book to it.

It doesn't matter where you are on your path toward your dreams, the point is you are probably further along than the person you are speaking with, and you know where you are going and how you are going to get there. Sometimes the fact that you haven't made it yet will help the other person relate to you sooner. The gap between where you are and where the other person is not so large that he or she can't see the possibilities.

Be open and honest about your story, and if you don't have one yet, admit it. Then ask if you can tell them a brief story about someone in the company you admire. They will understand and appreciate your honesty, adding heaps to your credibility as a person of integrity.

Heartfelt Network Marketing is about positive energy.

Excitement is catching; everyone wants some of it. Like moth to a flame, we are immediately attracted to another person's energy.

It is much more fun and exciting when people want to meet you and be around you. A happy person is an inspiration to everyone he or she meets.

Introduce your business the Heartfelt way.

Don't immediately call people you have not talked to in quite a while and start telling them about your new business. How would you like it if someone did this to you? If you have not communicated for years and then out of the blue you call them about the opportunity, you come across as cold and thoughtless, even if your intention was good. I am guilty of doing this, and it didn't feel good, which is why I am warning you not to do it.

However, sometimes you simply can't say the wrong thing to the right person.

You can only effectively introduce the business to someone you have already developed a relationship with, which means you know a little about their dreams and any pain they may be experiencing.

Relationship building happens faster as you develop your people and communication skills. In some cases, you can build rapport almost instantly, and in other cases, it might be an uphill battle. Studying books on body language will help you a great deal. Most people will tell you more through their body language and eyes than their words. A prospect leaning in toward you is always a great positive sign that you are connecting.

Remember to ask permission to share your story or information regarding products or services and the business. Ask permission to talk about how you may be able to help the prospect achieve his or her dreams or ease his or her pain.

When a prospect agrees to hearing what you have to say, try to start out with a story that leads into your business. If you sense that your prospect is uneasy talking about network marketing, don't argue with the person or defend the industry, just request that he or she keep an open mind for a few minutes and proceed with your human interest story.

You don't have to close at your first meeting, but don't leave prospects confused about your product and the business. The object is to open channels of communication. Give them time and work in an open relationship. They should feel that they can call and ask you questions without you subjecting them to a sales pitch.

Closing a sale today is not important; be relaxed and sharing and they will buy tomorrow.

Keep in mind that your prospect is more than just a sale. Your prospect could be interested in what you have to say because he or she is personally interested in the benefits of your offering and may become a product user. A happy product user is a gold mine, because often she will refer friends to you and in time your user or her friends may become interested in the business.

Your prospect may want to know about the business. If so, ask what aspect of growing a business interests him the most. Provide him with a few topics to select from and, in doing so, you are probably going to give him some ideas he may not yet have thought of.

Sometimes a prospect's needs or interests are not a good fit with your offering, and that is perfectly fine; if you have developed a good rapport with her, she may become a great supporter and advocate for you.

Most prospects want what network marketing offers, but they often tend to hesitate. Why is this? Generally it is due to the fear of the unknown, the fear of failure, and the fear of what others will say if they are unsuccessful. These three fears keep many prospects from getting started. It is great if you can relay some of your own fearful moments at the beginning and describe how you reacted and eventually overcame them.

Finally, remember to give value to your prospects; answer their questions openly and honestly. Don't make shallow promises or provide solutions to problems they don't have.

Heartfelt Network Marketing is about sharing, not selling.

Heartfelt Network Marketing is not in the business of scaring, confusing, or overwhelming people. We are concerned about people. The Heartfelt Network Marketing approach eventually gets people and prospects to start thinking seriously about their life and future.

Don't take it to heart if people don't come to your events. A mentor once said to me that opportunities and events are like cookies; you can offer them, and it is up to the individual to decide if he or she wants a cookie or not.

We are not emotionally attached to the outcome of our offer, because we are not selling—we are sharing. Don't strong-arm people or interrogate them on their excuses for not wanting to listen to you or declining an invitation to an event. We are sharing what worked for us and thousands of others, and it simply may not fit with them, or more importantly, it may not be the right time.

Some people will come for the cookies and the social interaction. They may never develop the business side, and that is perfectly OK. However, don't turn your back on these people. You know it works, and there may come a day when your cookie eater has a change of heart, in which case you want to be the person he or she seeks out.

One to two percent of the people who take the cookies will be interested in developing the business side of things, and that is all you need to become successful.

Heartfelt Network Marketing is more about asking questions and actively listening to the answers. Sometimes talking too much can put people off, and then they miss out on what it is you want to share with them.

Remember, we are here to share information, not hard sell. If your prospect is not interested in the business, then drop it immediately and change the subject. Don't reintroduce it at any time in the future—wait for him or her to ask you.

Heartfelt Network Marketing is not a hard-sell process—if someone disagrees with me, I graciously accept his or her point of view, and if it is appropriate, I ask if I may tell my story (and then I only relay the part of my story that relates to that person's issue). This is a storytelling business.

Heartfelt Network Marketing is about fulfilling your dreams through helping others to fulfill theirs.

There is no end to growing a successful business with the Heartfelt Network Marketing way, because there is no end to the line of people who need help. There is also no mandatory retirement and no end to the enjoyment when people you have nurtured fulfill their dreams.

Heartfelt Network Marketing improves your quality of life and possibly even the length of your wonderful life.

Heartfelt Dreaming, Hope, and the Ugly Alternative

> *Hope is the power that gives a person the confidence to step out and try.*
>
> —Zig Ziglar

Dreams Encourage You to Live and Grow

Dreaming is more than creating fanciful pictures in your head and sticking images of things you like on the bathroom mirror.

Heartfelt dreaming is powerful. It will help clear your mind and motivate you to action, leaving any feelings of depression, hopelessness, and impotence in the dust. Heartfelt dreams are powered by *hope* and backed up with a big enough *why* to keep you moving toward your dream.

If we just have a big enough why, and we're committed, we can accomplish great things in our life.

> *I want you to dream full out with intention and your heart.*

The Heartfelt way is to start out by asking questions. I want you to take a few minutes and answer the following questions about your dreaming and goals, and I don't mean your nighttime sleep dreams or wishful thinking:

- Do you have dreams and goals?

- If you do:
    - Can you easily recall what they are?
    - How do you feel when you think about them?
    - Have you got a plan to achieve your dreams?
    - Are you working on your plan?
    - Are you having fun working toward your dreams?
    - Do you need help to reach your dreams?

- If you don't have dreams and goals:
    - Can you remember a time when you did?
    - If you can, what were they?
    - What happened to your dreams?
    - How does it feel not having dreams and goals?
    - Why don't you have dreams and goals?
    - Do other people around you have dreams?

I have asked you these questions simply to get you focused on your dreams…or lack thereof. This is about you and your life going forward. I am already living some of my dreams and having fun creating new ones.

Dreams are personal, and they are free. There is no "use by" date to your dreams. Even if you haven't dreamed for a long time, you can start again anytime you want. However, this time you want your dreams to come from your heart and your mind, and to help you I have outlined a few steps later in this chapter.

Dreams get your engine started and hope empowers you to go on the adventure. Dreams take on a new meaning when there is hope. Hope gives you the strength to push through fear and ridicule. Hope fuels your passion for life on your terms. While you have hope, you will continue to find ways to go forward.

Dreaming and knowing how to turn your dreams into reality is one of the most exciting skills you will ever possess; from that point forward, your life becomes an adventure designed by you for you and your family.

One of your most rewarding roles as a heartfelt network marketer is to shine a light for others and help them dream and hope again, but you have to walk the talk yourself first.

We all need a glimmer of hope and a dream to strive for. I don't know what your dreams are, but if they require a strong sense of self-worth, courage, personal growth, imagination, passion, support from like-minded people, and money, then network marketing could be the hope you are looking for. This industry is built on personal development and supporting each other in achieving our dreams. Nearly everyone I talk to at a company meeting can tell me instantly about their dreams and how they are getting there.

Heartfelt Network Marketing teaches you how to help others achieve their dreams while you are achieving yours. Your dreams can be as exciting and far-reaching as climbing the ten highest mountains in the world, or they can be as small as going to bed at night without eating that last piece of cake. There is no law that says dreams must be larger than life or that some dreams are better than others. No one has the right to cast judgment on your dreams, but they can wholeheartedly support you on your journey.

Another wonderful thing about dreams is that they can and sometimes do change over time. Sometimes your situation changes, and this alters your dream, and that's all right because they are your dreams and you decide their shape and color. At the start I dreamed of paying my bills and taking a family vacation.

The thought of one day becoming a millionaire and owning a multimillion-dollar business was not in my frame of reference, but as I grew and the business grew, so have my dreams.

I want you to hope and dream. Don't settle for less than you deserve, and don't let others stop you from dreaming and hoping. You need your dreams. Dream with emotion. Feel it, see the color, hear the sounds, and create the stories. Your subconscious buys into imagery and feelings. Turn your dreams into a wonderful, colorful, emotion-packed, all-singing-and-dancing movie in your mind.

Dreams are more powerful than you may have thought. These are some of the words I associate with dreams:

- Inspiration
- Direction
- Motivation
- Happiness
- Strength
- Excitement
- Work
- Fun
- Purpose
- Achievement
- Control
- Energy
- Feeling great
- Role model
- Helping others

Conversely, I can remember a time when I didn't dream and aspire to creating a life on my terms, and these are some of the words and feelings that come to mind:

- Helpless
- Hopeless
- Bored
- Depressed
- Impotence
- Needy
- Tired
- Mundane
- Just getting older
- Out of my control
- Poor role model
- Why bother
- Who cares
- Defeated

The point is that your dreams are personal. You create them and, unfortunately, you can also lose sight or give up on them. How many dreams do you have sitting in the "too hard" basket, or worse, in the trash?

The Ugly Alternative

I know from personal experience how life can erode dreams like the wind turns cliffs into sand on the beach. Our dreams turn to sand so slowly that we don't notice or feel it happening until one day we turn around and ask ourselves, "What was that?" That was our life.

Life can wear you down sometimes and sap the energy right out from under you. At the time it seems that there is nothing you can do about it. I know how debilitating life can get at times. I think I was living in an ongoing cycle of ups and downs with depression and financial stress for at least twenty years of my forty-plus years at the time.

Do you remember having dreams and aspirations years ago when you were in school or starting out on your first day at work or college? What happened to those dreams? Or are you one of the fortunate ones who managed to keep a hold of your dream and bring it to life?

I was a sensitive and shy young girl who liked to melt into the crowd. Unfortunately, I never quite managed to blend in as much as I wished. Through my entire school years, I dreamed of nothing else except dressing like the rest of the kids and fitting in. Mom used to make some beautiful clothes for my sister and me, but they never looked store-bought, and when you are a kid that's all that matters. I always felt different and just not in the same class as the others. My dream of fitting in eventually turned into a belief that I was not quite enough, and this sat on my shoulders for the next thirty years.

A few years ago, I learned that I was not the only family member to suffer from unfulfilled dreams. My father was a very hard worker, driving trucks in the snow and buses across the country, and many years after he died, my mother told me that he had really wanted to be a pilot. Unfortunately he never had the opportunity to even hope that one day he would realize his dream. He was a handsome, charismatic man who told the best stories imaginable and was known for keeping his passengers amused and entertained on their long bus rides.

I wish he had known about network marketing, because he would have been brilliant at it. He would have easily achieved financial freedom, which would have given him the means to live his dream of flying above the clouds.

I am sure you could tell a similar story about someone dear to you or even relate to this story a little bit yourself. The greatest difference between my father's dream and yours is that you still have time to reach your dream.

Sometimes events out of our control keep us from dreaming. The year before I entered the network marketing industry was one of those times. I became overwhelmed by helplessness and my mortality. Three people close to me were going through immense pain as breast cancer, leukemia, and brain tumors wracked their lives.

My very close friend Polly was dying of cancer, and she was only forty-eight when she died; she was just seven years older than me. A group of us took turns looking after her for one day a week. I would take Polly to her chemo sessions and then sit by her bed sharing stories and fun memories. She would say to me with such finality that "it is plain and simple; I am going to die." I would leave overwhelmed by our mortality.

Not long after I started to care for Polly, Angela, another close girlfriend of ours, learned that her young son, Mario, had an aggressive brain tumor. This devastated all of us. Mario underwent three horrendous brain operations within a few months, but unfortunately they could not save him, and he died at the age of ten. If that wasn't enough heartache, another girlfriend's baby boy, Micah, was diagnosed with leukemia. Micah died at the age of six, a few years younger than my son Nathan. I couldn't imagine how I would cope knowing that my little boy was dying and there was nothing I could do but hold him.

Polly died in November, followed by Mario in May, and then Micah six months later. I hadn't really thought too much about life and death until that year. Being so close to all of this real life misery brought home to me that life is very short and we don't know what lies in wait for us or our loved ones. Throughout this time I felt so helpless. I supported my friends emotionally, but I didn't have the finances to help them in any other way. I couldn't help with their medical bills or even help with small things to make their final days a little more comfortable. It didn't matter how much we cried and held each other, we were helpless to change the outcome.

The feeling of total helplessness and watching friends around my own age dying without ever having been free, or little ones who never had a chance to become teenagers, was just way too much for me. I didn't have the heart to dream; I just continued living in sadness and burying myself further into debt and work.

I now know that there is nothing to be gained by giving in to what life throws at you.

Living a life in which you feel it is hopeless to try and you feel beaten before you even start is miserable for you and those around you, but there is a way out. I was drowning in misery and frustration for most of my life, and by a simple twist of fate, I found a heartfelt way to my dreams.

A year after our community was devastated by death, Joni took me to my first network marketing meeting. It was a different world to the one I had been living in. I saw other ordinary people creating a future, and I wanted that with a vengeance. I didn't ever want to have that feeling of total financial helplessness ever again. I wanted the freedom to experience life and to have the money to help my family and friends with whatever came our way. I had found my "big enough why" and a way to get there. The why was so strong that it empowered me to overcome my fear of starting something I knew very little about and to ignore the ridicule and jokes from friends and family who didn't understand my drive. I believed that nothing could be as devastating as the feeling of helplessness that came from watching loved ones die without ever having experienced freedom to live a life of their making. The night of my very first network marketing meeting, I started to dream again, and this time I knew with all my heart that I was going to make it.

Going from Depressed to Dreaming

Hope is incredibly powerful. It can bring long lost dreams to life in an instant. That first network marketing meeting instantly reignited my excitement for life and dreaming. Everything came back to life within minutes, and Joni and I started to dream big dreams before we even left our seats. Listening to ordinary people like us talk about their dreams and how they are getting closer every day, and how some of them have even exceeded their wildest dreams through network marketing, was totally inspiring. I had an epiphany there and then.

I can do this—I can dream and get there!

The first dream we both had was to retire our husbands. Both men worked in unfulfilling jobs in very difficult environments, and we wanted to set them free. Todd is Joni's husband, and the vision of the day he retired from the mill motivated Joni to take control of her life and get moving with serious intention.

I remember with much joy the day Todd retired. It was cause for a great party. With the help of Joni's young sons, we planned a surprise party, starting with picking Todd up at the end of his shift on his last day at the mill. I rented a Hummer limo and seventeen of us drove around town wearing oversized sunglasses and drinking champagne. We were dressed in our best and dined at a fancy restaurant on the water. We even stayed overnight at a lodge in Puget Sound, near Shelton.

It was a wonderful, fun time, because Joni's first major dream had come true. She had retired her husband at fifty, after he'd worked in the local mill for thirty years as a lumber sorter. Only a few years later, two guys doing the job he did were killed on the line. That could easily have been Todd.

I will always remember the night we drove up in the limo to pick Todd up at the end of his final day. He had the biggest grin on his face as we escorted him toward the long, white stretch limo to the tune of the theme from *Rocky*. The other lumbermen continued to shuffle along to their cars with their heads down. Not one of the men congratulated Todd. It was depressing to see these hardworking men so overwhelmed with hopelessness that they couldn't even be happy for one of their own who had escaped and was now living his dream.

Dreams are visions of our destination, and hope is the fuel needed to get there.

Bringing Your Heartfelt Dreams into Reality

Now it's time to do some work on your future. I want you to pack all your limiting beliefs, pet debilitating phrases, trials and tribulations of the past, and worries about the future into a suitcase and leave it at the door. Don't worry—no one is going to steal your luggage, and you can pick it up again at the end, but be warned: you might want to leave it there.

Approach this heartfelt dreaming process with an open heart and an attitude of "What if?" I know you seriously can't start with a blank piece of paper because you have a life already, and you probably have family commitments, but you can wonder what things would be like if you found a way to make it possible.

The best way to do this is to leave your history and doubts, your prejudices and fears, behind, if only for a few hours. We are talking about you creating a gift for yourself and your loved ones, and that takes heartfelt intention, clarity of thought, and an open state of mind.

The following is a simple six-step strategy to creating a dream and turning it into reality. There are hundreds of books on the subject, which you can research later, but I want you to get started now. So here is the essence to creating, planning, and achieving your heartfelt dreams.

> **1. The What and Why**
> **2. The When**
> **3. Documenting Your Dream**
> **4. The Plan**
> **5. The Price**
> **6. The Secret Sauce**

If you are married or have a special loved one in your life, I strongly recommend getting them involved in this process. Creating dreams and bringing them to life is a commitment, and your chances of success are far greater if both of you, and your family, are headed in the same direction with the same intention.

On the other hand, if your spouse or significant other isn't interested or doesn't have the time, get going anyway. Don't try to get it absolutely perfect the first time around; just get it done.

If you don't know where you are going, you're not going to like where you wind up.

—*Jim Brooks*

---

1. The What and Why

Start your journey with your dream—if you don't know where you want to go, anywhere will do.

Your degree of success is far greater if you blend your why and your dream together. I suggest that you start by creating a shopping list of the things you want and build it up from there. Your first round could be as simple as:

- Start my own business
- Get to the gym more than once a week
- Become debt-free
- Buy a new car
- Take the kids on a vacation to Disneyland this year
- Always have my clothes clean and ready to wear
- Give up smoking forever
- Start college funds for grandchildren as they are born
- Join a brilliant mastermind group
- Adopt a child from a third-world country
- Spend more time with my spouse
- Know the meaning of my life
- Hire an assistant or nanny

This is your Heartfelt Dream List. Review this list several times and write down the reasons why each dream is important to you. If you can't think of a genuine, heartfelt reason worth writing down, move that item to your Wish List and forget about it for the time being. Reviewing your Heartfelt Dream List is a repetitive process. Keep going through the list until you understand the truth about what you want and why. The longer you work on it, the deeper you will dig, and eventually you will start to come up with the really *big* whys.

This step could easily take you a couple of weeks, and you should consider asking your spouse and children for their input as well. Children have dreams you may not be aware of; by learning what they are, perhaps you might help them achieve their dreams. When my youngest son, Nathan, was fifteen, he was passionate about acting. He dreamed about going to New York and attending a special two-week acting course that everyone was talking about. Fortunately, he shared his dream with me, and by then, my residual income was enough that I was able to pay for him to attend the eight-day acting class and auditions in New York. To make it even better, I was able to accompany him and we created incredible memories together.

I have to admit that before my Heartfelt Network Marketing days, I remember not helping my kids to dream and sometimes even squashing them. One time, Justin asked, "Do artists make a lot of money?"

I said, "No. Many of them are called starving artists."

I didn't realize the power I had over his dream. Later, he asked about becoming a diver, and this frightened me because I thought this was a dangerous occupation. I somehow convinced him to drop that dream as well. As a parent, sometimes we are too quick to shut down our children's dreams. Fortunately, Heidi dreamed of a college education and had the common sense to ignore my lack of money at the time. She put herself through college and created a very successful career in the arts; sadly, she did it with very little help from me.

The object is to get down to one or two fundamental reasons why you want what you want. Two key passions in my life are to be free and to help as many people as I can to live their dreams.

If you are having trouble coming up with your list of heartfelt dreams, I suggest you stop and look into your future. A few years ago, a glimpse of what my future might have been presented itself when I walked into a hair salon in town to have my hair done. I saw a sight that took me back in time—the salon owner had rented out stations to a group of very elderly stylists, many of the clients using walkers and wheelchairs to get around. Although I really admired their work ethic and wondered if it was their passion for their art that kept them going; deep down I knew they were still working because they needed to. Sadly, in a matter of only a few months, the salon owner moved them all out, and they were homeless just before Christmas, which is always a very busy time for older clients.

...Where will you be 20 years from now?

I was taken aback by the whole experience and thanked my Heartfelt Network Marketing business, because that could easily have been me down the road. The only difference was that I would have been wearing a back brace and using a walker.

To help you get some clarity, sometimes you need to have a serious look at where your future is heading. Ask yourself some questions about the future, and if your spouse is working on your dream design with you, ask for his or her input as well. It will be interesting to see if you have similar or very different views on the future; that in itself is a good thing to know.

Some questions to get you started are:

- If you do nothing different, what will your life be like this same time next year, three years, five years, or ten years?
- If you keep on doing nothing different, what will your life be like five years, ten years, and twenty years from now?
- What will life be like as a grandparent with no time and money to spend with your grandchildren?
- What will it be like living on social security, if it even exists then?
- What will it be like if your children's families have moved away and you don't have the means to travel to see them and your grandchildren?
- Will retirement be a blessing or a nightmare?
- What will it be like if you don't look after your health?
- How will you cope if your pension isn't sufficient to cover your retirement?

Sorry about this, but these are some of the hard questions in life that you may want to ask yourself when you are working on your heartfelt dreams. It is said that we will do more to avoid pain than seek pleasure, so this is what you are doing now. You are working on the probable painful alternative if you don't do something *now*.

When you are happy that you have a shortlist of dreams supported by passionate reasons why, it is time to ask yourself a few more questions about each item. These are some great questions I discovered in John C. Maxwell's book, *Put Your Dream to the Test*:

- Is my dream really my dream?
- Do I clearly see my dream?
- Am I depending on factors within my control to achieve my dream?
- Does my dream compel me to follow it?
- Does my dream benefit others?

John says that the more yes answers you come up with the greater your chances are of success. This makes a lot of sense to me for several reasons:

- If it isn't *your dream*, you are more likely to drop out when the going gets tough.
- If you can't see your dream clearly, you might lose your way over time—like getting lost in the forest at night.
- If your dream is subject to factors outside your control, you are in a high-risk game, but keep going.
- If your dream isn't truly compelling, you may not have the courage and energy to see it through.
- If your dream benefits others, especially your children, you have reasons why that far exceeds yourself and that will inspire you to push through.

2. The When

Never give up on a dream just because of the time it will take to accomplish it. The time will pass anyway.

—Earl Nightingale

You probably have a number of dreams or at least one dream with a lot of smaller parts. Either way, prioritize each dream or part and work out if some things need to be achieved before others. In other words, create a sequence of events.

You may also have some schedules that are outside of your control, and your problem will be how to get the task performed to match the schedule. For example, you might want to attend a network marketing company event with a set registration date, or you might want to qualify for a company competition, so you need to work with that deadline.

Other dreams may not have a hard and fast schedule, and that is perfectly fine because it is *your* dream and you get to call the shots.

3. Documenting Your Dream

A picture is worth a thousand words.

This is the second most important step in your dream creation process. Commit your dream to paper and create a vision board. A vision board is simply a large piece of paper covered with pictures and photos of your dreams. Hang the board up in a prominent place where you will see it regularly throughout the day. This will be a great, colorful constant reminder of why you are doing what you are doing.

It will keep you on track, and when the going gets tough, your description and images of your dream will inspire you with absolute clarity. This is your journey and destination.

I suggest that when you are writing up your dreams you describe how you feel about your dreams, how you will feel when you are there, and how you feel right now. Feelings are a large part of what you are doing, and your subconscious responds well to feelings.

Another great modality is to record your descriptions and feelings about your heartfelt dreams. You can then listen to your own dreams and aspirations while driving to work or working out at the gym. Intersperse your own recordings with some of the great personal development gurus and you will be surprised at how focused you become.

After listening to your voice describing your dreams a few times, you may even go back to the dream design board and make some enhancements or refinements. If you do, it would be a good move to rerecord your revised dreams.

So there you have it. Your dreams will be written up, represented on a vision board and in your ear. You won't be able to get away from your dreams.

4. The Plan

Empty pockets never held anyone back. Only empty heads and empty hearts can do that.

—*Norman Vincent Peale*

This is where you will create an overall plan for how to get from where you are now to your dream destination. Plans are very dynamic and take on a life of their own as we work through them. They are not set in stone. It is not unusual for plans to be modified from time to time to allow for changing circumstances, but the point is you have a plan or strategy in place so you can get started.

You need a road map to show you the way to your heartfelt dreams. If you can't plan all the way at first, just start with what you can do and build on it as you go.

When you are working out your plan, make it exciting enough that your spouse and children will want to work with you. There are no free rides to your dream destination, and remember, you can't steer a parked car. So get moving.

At the start, I was not the best planner, and I found that working in the network marketing industry and mixing with the top achievers helped me a great deal. I didn't have to start my plan from scratch. I was able to discuss my dreams with people who had already reached their dreams and benefit from their wisdom and guidance. This is another great advantage to belonging to a professional industry group—there is always a pool of people and experience to draw from.

5. The Price

There is only one way to avoid criticism: do nothing, say nothing, and be nothing.

—*Aristotle*

A wise man once said to me that there is no such thing as a free lunch, and I have found him to be right on the money. Now I am telling you that there is no such thing as a free dream, and this is from experience.

Everything in life has a price. It could be financial, time, energy, pain, pleasure—absolutely anything, but it will be there. The trick is to work out what the price is and ask yourself if you are willing to pay it. This is why it is so very important for you to have designed your heartfelt dream with the utmost care and attention.

Throughout my career as a Heartfelt Network Marketer, I have undergone a lifetime of continual personal development and learning. I love attending courses, masterminds, company events, and team workshops. Sometimes I am in the audience taking piles of notes, and on other occasions I am on the stage. Traveling is a large part of my network marketing business, and it is imperative that I look professional at all times, even waiting at LAX for a flight that is already six hours late. My profession is helping people, and they are everywhere, so my goal is to be prepared. My ongoing education and business development are tangible costs like any other type of business expense—they may be unavoidable but at least they are tax deductible.

The great thing about belonging to a network marketing company is that often the company will sponsor great motivational speakers and events you can attend for free or for a fraction of what it might cost the general public.

Sometimes the price is not money but time and opportunities. These are not so easy to watch out for unless you have a great plan in place. Unfortunately, as a young wife and mother, I didn't realize that I was paying a price for my hunger to succeed. Looking back, I now realize that I inadvertently volunteered my husband and children to also pay a price. I thought that I was doing the best job I could by working long hours, helping to keep us financially afloat, and building my business.

A typical Wednesday night, I would work up until nine o'clock and conduct a phone team call at eight o'clock while I was still shampooing or cutting hair. Sometimes I would even end up recruiting my eight o'clock client after the call. The Wednesday night team call is still going on today…minus the shampooing. It was very exciting, as it was a commitment to our future.

The price seemed very small to me at the time, probably because there were lots of little payments over time and it wasn't until the end that it tallied up to be pretty expensive. I didn't realize at the time that my eldest son was heading down a path that eventually led him to an addiction that became bigger then he was. He was a young man and fortunately when he was ready to be saved, Heidi and I were able to get him into a leading rehab clinic within the next twenty-four hours. It was my residual income that made it possible to keep him in rehab long enough for him to make a full recovery. I often wonder whether, if I had spent more time with him as a youngster, he might have avoided the drug problem altogether. Of course, hindsight is twenty-twenty.

I rarely took time to go on family reunions and trips when the rest of the family did. I believed that I couldn't go because of my commitment to my clients, but I did have a choice, and I chose to work in the salon instead. Eventually, my husband and our marriage paid the ultimate price of divorce.

Looking back, the price I paid was far bigger than I knew, and I don't recommend that you throw yourself into building your dreams until you have worked out exactly what you are building, why you are building it, and what it will cost you and your loved ones.

The lesson I want to pass on to you is that sometimes a price is paid unknowingly and it could be high. If you take the time to design your dream with care and go through the steps outlined above, you will have a much greater chance of making a decision you and your family will be happy to live with.

6. The Secret Sauce

Unfortunately, it doesn't matter how wonderful our dreams are or how meticulously we have created our plan—it is all just a story until we put it into action.

The secret is a four letter word: WORK. In fact, it is HEART WORK.

When I started on my path to freedom, I worked at my day job, and I worked on my network marketing business two nights a week and a few hours on the weekend. I listened to personal development tapes nonstop and read as many books as I could get my hands on. We didn't have Amazon back then, but Joni found our first set of network marketing books, called *Big Al Tells All*, for a dollar at a garage sale, and we shared them with our team

Work also meant showing up to as many local and company meetings as possible. I never missed a large event, even though I often charged the whole trip on our credit cards. I always saw it as an investment in my future. I figured that it was worth every minute and every cent to be among these amazingly successful people that I would normally never have meet.

At these meetings, I could listen to their stories and learn from them.

I used every opportunity to meet the top achievers and build relationships with them. I would ask them questions about how they did it and what they would do when they were confronted with all kinds of issues.

Remember, there is no such thing as a free heartfelt dream; however, the price you end up paying for the ugly alternative is always a lot higher. We are talking about your life, your future, and the legacy you will leave for your family.

Wrap Up

Dreaming mixed with your drive and passion to help others will set you on the path to freedom—freedom to breathe, freedom to grow, freedom to create inspiring relationships, freedom to wonder, freedom to chase adventures, freedom to learn, freedom to help your family and friends, freedom to help people less fortunate, freedom from financial chains, freedom to have the time to be loving, freedom to be actively involved with your children and grandchildren, and simply freedom to look up and see the wonderful world you live in.

Your growing self-confidence will help you overcome the ridicule others may throw your way. You have to make your own decisions and dream your own life—don't let others tear down your dreams just because they don't understand or don't want you to put in the work. It's like the dog chasing the rabbit story.

People see the dog chasing the rabbit but they don't see the rabbit, so they think the dog has gone crazy.

As you start to experience success, your dreams become bigger. Your belief that you can turn your dreams into reality grows, and your dreams grow with it. Fear and uncertainty soon become past memories.

My powers of visualization and dreaming grew with each success I achieved. My first step was buying a newer car, and then I bought my first house as a single mom. The incredible warm feeling of financial independence and owning my very own home after my divorce will be with me forever.

Leave your luggage at the door, and don't let others stop you from going through those red doors! Watch out for the dream snatchers.

Twenty years from now you will be more disappointed by the things that you didn't do than the ones you did do.

—*Mark Twain*

The Fundamentals of the Network Marketing Industry

The number one guideline to success is you must be in business for yourself. When you work for someone else, you sell your time at wholesale to your employer, who then resells it at retail to the customer.

—J. Paul Getty

We are all network marketers in our everyday lives, but not everyone receives a check for their recommendations. Most of your life, you have been recommending to your friends which restaurants, movies, diets, and dentists you think they would like. Even as a child, you probably recommended cartoons and candy to your school pals; I know I did. Unless you were under contract with the business that provided the product or service you were recommending, there is a good chance that they never sent you a check when your friend took up your recommendation, let alone when your friend recommended them to another friend.

Network marketing is a sales and marketing strategy in which you are rewarded for sharing the company's products or services and building a team of product distributors or service advocates to do likewise. Your team is a voluntary army of independent distributors and customers.

The network marketing business model is designed to benefit the company, the customer, and the distributor. The company benefits because it does not have to fund large advertising budgets and employee benefits for its vast sales division. The customer benefits because there is no middle man adding a margin onto the price of the products because it comes directly from the company. The distributor benefits by sharing the products and services and building a business made up of happy product users and sharers. The sales and marketing savings allow the company to maintain a high level of investment in the making of high-quality products.

Network Marketing Is a Business

This is a real business. It is not a get rich quick scheme, and it is not a hobby…unless you want it to be.

Becoming a network marketing professional involves a commitment to personal growth, time, and patience. You get back what you put into it. It is not a free ride. Think about how long it takes for a person to become a CPA, teacher, counselor, or any other profession. It generally takes four to six years of college to get to the point where someone can start to practice a vocation and earn an income. Even after years of study, workers start at the entry level of their profession on a fairly ordinary annual salary.

The difference with becoming a professional network marketer is that you get paid while you are learning, and you can start building your team and business from the start. The quickest way to learn and improve is to get out and do it. Network marketing enables you to start applying your lessons as soon as you feel comfortable. You are the CEO of your business from day one.

This profession pays you to learn and grow.

In his book **Outliers**: *The Story of Success, author Malcolm Gladwell says that it takes roughly ten thousand hours of practice to achieve mastery in a field.*

Ten thousand hours equates to about two hundred and fifty standard working weeks, or five years. This, according to Gladwell, is the time required to reach mastery, and I think that's about right for a professional network marketer to truly walk the talk. However, I have met people in the industry who have achieved mastery much more quickly.

Here is a great story from one of my mentors, Tom "Big Al" Schreiter, that shows why most businesses take time to build.

The Casino

Let's say Donald Trump wants to build a casino in your hometown. The first year is spent looking for a location and securing a building site. Next, Donald creates a public relations campaign about the casino and the jobs it will create so that the local residents will support the project instead of resisting the construction. After the successful public relations campaign, Donald starts negotiating with the local government for permits, licenses, and building approvals. After twelve months of negotiations and hearings, the casino project is approved by the city council. Bids are put out to contractors for the construction of the casino. After reviewing the bids, construction can start. First, a giant hole is dug into the ground for the foundation of the megacasino. Three months of digging creates a huge hole. Donald comes by the next day to review his progress. He walks up to the big hole in the ground, looks down, and says, "I quit. I have spent three years on this project and haven't earned a penny yet!" Do you really think Donald would say that? Of course not. He is a successful businessman. He knows he has to build the casino first before he can start earning money. So Donald finishes his casino project even though he hasn't earned a penny yet. When the casino is finished, it is an enormous cash generator. Money and profits pour in day after day after day for years and years.

Be realistic; you may not generate any income for the first few months, but sooner or later you will. It is exciting to receive checks in the mail rather than just bills. Network marketing pays you on what you do. You don't have to wait to be promoted. Provided that you continue to work your business and grow your team, you will find those little checks begin to turn into big checks.

Your regular job pays for your regular bills and lifestyle—your part-time networking check can pay for your future.

Treat your network marketing business as a great part-time business until you reach the point where your part-time income matches or exceeds your regular income. At this point in time, you may want to consider going full time. It took me eleven years and five companies before I stepped through the Red Doors to go from hairdresser and part-time network marketer to full-time professional networker, and I have never looked back.

There Is Income and Then There Is Residual Income

The main difference between building a network marketing business and working in a regular business is your income stream. Provided you have put in the effort and built your team, your NM business will continue to generate income 24-7, even while you are on vacation, in the hospital, at the movies, asleep, or simply slowing down. As an employee of a company, you only get paid when you are working. Of course, you may also be paid for two weeks' vacation a year and a few days' sick leave, but the bottom line is you are and will always be a work for hire person.

Think about the CEO of a multinational company who is taking home a million dollars a year while working for a regular company. This sounds great, but can they call in and tell the board that they will be working from Hawaii for the next three months or cutting their hours down to fifteen hours a week with no pay cut? Network marketing can give you the freedom to choose your work hours and location.

If you were a successful novelist or an actor in a TV commercial, you would receive money every time your book sold or your advertisement was aired. This is called *residual income*. It is quite different from regular income, which is sometimes referred to as *linear income*. Linear income continues only as long as you continue the work, and in some instances it is even dependent on you actually achieving some agreed outcome.

When I was sitting in the audience at my first network marketing meeting, I realized that no matter how hard I worked at my hair salon or how many hairstyling competitions I won, there was never going to be a residual income stream and financial freedom. Residual income simply was not part of the profession I had been working hard in since I was sixteen.

I can personally attest to the wonders of residual income and this profession. A few years ago, I was talking on my cell phone and didn't notice the marble stairs as I walked off them in platform high heels. I slipped on the first step and reached out to the handrail to try to break my fall. The next thing I knew I was being rushed to the ER. My arm was ultimately in a cast for six weeks. Thanks to my networking business, my income didn't miss a beat.

Would this happen in a regular employee situation? It certainly would not have happened had I still been a hairdresser. I would have been out of work for at least three to four months and out of money.

In many companies, your network marketing business can be included in your estate and willed to your family. Can your regular job keep paying your family after you have gone?

You Get to Choose the People You Work With

This is your business, so you get to decide who you will work with in your downline. You get to choose who you will help to develop and grow their business.

I am so passionate about helping people that on occasion I have fallen for the trap of spending a great deal of my time and money on helping people who are not willing to help themselves. These days I am a little wiser, so before I get too involved I give them a small task. If they follow through, I will work with them further, but if they don't deliver, I will wait for them to raise their hand when they are ready. I have virtually unlimited time and patience for passionate hard workers, for these are the people who are hungry to learn and grow and just need a helping hand.

You also get to choose the products and services you want to work with, as well as when, where, and how you work. I work with a product I love and people who have become my friends. Remember, in network marketing you work *for* yourself but not *by* yourself.

Network Marketing Is an Equal Opportunity Business

Network marketing can work for anyone. There is no glass ceiling or gender bias. There is no discrimination of any kind. There is no racism or ageism. It works just as well for disabled and able-bodied people. If you have hearing and speech impediments, you can still find a way to make it work, because there are no rules as to who can and cannot play the game.

Depending on which network marketing company you work with, you also have the option to go global, so once again, there are no boundaries to growing your business. It is a great business that rewards you for your efforts.

The following are examples of the types of people who have become involved in network marketing:

- Unemployed
- Entrepreneurs
- Stay-at-home moms
- Full-time corporate workers
- Teachers and students
- Doctors and lawyers
- Shop keepers and accountants
- Retired people and top sports stars
- Millionaires and people struggling financially
- Young and old people
- Men and women

Personally, I have always found stay-at-home moms, teachers, hairdressers, coaches, and nurses make the greatest Heartfelt Network Marketers. They start from a position of wanting to help others.

This Is a Business Nonetheless

This is a real business, which obviously means there is a chance that you can fail financially.

In order to partake in prosperity you have to participate in prosperity.

—*Jimmy Smith*

Network marketing is like a board game—you have to play the game to win, and sometimes you will jump ahead while other times you will have to take it one step at a time.

Like all games in life, you need to weigh the pros and cons from your perspective. Nobody else can do it for you, because we are talking about your life, your future, your dreams, your hopes, and your fears. Don't let anyone steal them. They belong to you.

I started my dreaming a lifetime ago, and over the past few years I have been able to cross some of them off my list. It started with simply things like being able to catch a cab instead of calling a friend or relative for a lift, buying a condo for my beautiful mother, saving my son's life and putting my youngest son through LSU without a student loan. Thanks to my residual income, I was able to pay for my son to stay in rehab for four and a half months, way longer than any state program would do.

There are also less obvious benefits to running your own network marketing business—tax benefits, for example. Here is a priceless story about a friend of mine who, many years ago, was having trouble convincing her husband that network marketing was the way to go.

Angela Cruz and I were both hairdressers, and I worked in her salon for a while when my youngest boy was six months old. I introduced Angela to network marketing, and at first she was reluctant, but I wanted her to join me because she was so much fun to be with. She started to come along to the meetings because she also enjoyed the fun. Eventually, she joined the first company with me and she worked at it just like I did. Neither of us made enough money to brag about from the first company, but we reaped many benefits in other ways, like our personal development, new friends, support, and enthusiasm. Her husband was against it and often questioned why she was spending time and money and not really making anything. Fortunately, one of her salon clients was also their CPA, and she said to Angela's husband, "Look, she may not be bringing in money, but you owe her $6,000 at the end of the year. You need to write her a check for how much she saved you by having a home-based business, so you owe her."

Another not-so-obvious benefit is personal development. You are paid to learn the business and to grow personally. Both of these rewards will also help everyone you come in contact with. You will be like the pebble in the pond, spreading hope and freedom.

Selecting the Right Company, Product, and Sponsor for You

Selecting the right company and the best sponsor for you is vital to the success of your network marketing career. When I stared out I didn't know what I was looking for. I was green in the industry, and I didn't know anything about the basics of network marketing.

I joined my first company by default. My friend Joni and I attended a local meeting and we became enthused by what we saw and heard, so we signed up immediately. The product wasn't life-changing for me, but it was exciting because of the people I met and the fact that many of them liked it.

Over the years, I have learned that there are some valuable questions to ask and research to do before joining a company. Take responsibility and see for yourself rather than listening to other people's advice. Here are a few things to consider:

- If you just join anything because it's the latest, greatest craze, then people have to question if you'd fall for anything. You have to believe in something or you'll fall for anything and everything, quickly losing your credibility.

- Do the company values align with your values? If you have your values all sorted out and it works for you and your family, and those values are held up by the company that you work for, whether traditional business or network marketing, then it's going to be a good ride. The first company I joined was an exciting company with proven benefits for those who used the products. I stayed with this company for three years and finally left due to an ethical conflict. Unfortunately, the top achievers manipulated team structures to benefit a chosen few, and I didn't agree with this type of behavior. The top achievers often gave us bad advice, which again benefited them and not necessarily us. Joni and I were newbies and were being taken advantage of; we felt like bird dogs sent out to collect names and warm up prospects and then turn them over to our upline, who lacked ethics. I realized that the company values did not match mine. I felt very sad about leaving this company. In a strange kind of way, I felt like I was going through a divorce. However, this was one of my first lessons that formed the foundation of Heartfelt Network Marketing—integrity and congruency between my beliefs and my actions are paramount.

- Go to a company event to see the kinds of people in the organization and meet the company owners. Ask yourself if they are the kind of people you want to be friends with.

- Talk to people who are already involved in the business.

- There are a wide variety of compensation plans. Check the compensation plan out thoroughly, making sure you seriously understand it and that it meets your criteria.

- Look into the company's back-office systems. A reputable company should have computer and warehouse systems capable of processing large volumes of orders and payments without a hiccup. Ask some of the existing company agents if they have experienced any issues with product delivery or their compensation checks.

- Would you use the company products or services even if you didn't represent the company? Look into the people who are responsible for creating the products and services. If the company manufactures products that rely on science, check out the credentials of the scientists the company employs.

- Are you able to be living proof that the products and services are valuable and work as advertised?

- Is the product visual? Personally, I prefer to work with products I can demonstrate visually. I find that it is easier to share my story if the people can see for themselves.

- Sometimes the company can let you down, as compared to the people letting you down. My short-lived career with my second company taught me this valuable lesson. I joined at the recommendation of a highly regarded networking friend. I did not do my own due diligence but simply followed and learned another valuable lesson. If the company fails, you are out of business in that company. Go find another company. Unfortunately, the company was closed down by the FTC within six months, which left all of us sitting on the curb. I was left hurt and embarrassed, but it was my own fault because I did not check things out thoroughly for myself before deciding to join.

- Many companies allow you to sell your business line or will it to your descendants. You are in it for the long haul. You may be able to develop enough residual income that it is worth more than the life insurance policy you are currently paying for.

- What kind of tools and systems for training are provided? Does the company have regular group calls and online videos, webinars, podcasts, and so forth? Are they utilizing the latest technology for expanding and building your business?

- Is there a ceiling to your growth?
- If you are serious about building a network marketing business, it would be wise to make sure your sponsor is also serious about growing the business. It is easier if you know your sponsor's level of commitment. (Note: It is a volunteer army, and sometimes sponsors leave. Don't be discouraged; just reach upline and find another leader to work with. Remember you are responsible for your own business.)

- Will the company culture suit you? I was looking for a family feel, and it took me five companies to get there.

The Heartfelt Network Marketing way is about integrity, and for me that means I have to believe in the company, the business opportunity, and the product. It is a nonnegotiable trio.

I had a gut feeling that my current company met all three of my selection criteria, so I tested it out. I took a couple of before photographs and purchased the thirty-day program. My gut instinct was right. I dropped three dress sizes within thirty days, and I didn't need to hard sell this company and the product because my clients could see what was happening, and they wanted in on the "secret." I also met the owners face-to-face early on, and that was very important. I could see into their eyes when we talked, and I felt even more comfortable that I had selected the right company for me.

Network Marketing Myths

If you are new to network marketing, you will no doubt come across a lot of information and misinformation regarding the industry. You owe it to yourself to really check things out thoroughly before joining a company. However, there are some issues I feel I should shed some light on based on my seventeen years of experience in this profession.

Myth #1: They Are All Pyramid Schemes

There are hundreds of definitions of a pyramid scheme, and they basically come down to this: a pyramid scheme is an unsustainable business model that involves promising participants payment or services primarily for enrolling other people into the scheme rather than for supplying any real investment or sale of products or services to the public.

Pyramid schemes are illegal in the United States and in most other countries, including Australia, Canada, China, New Zealand, Norway, the Philippines, Sweden, and the United Kingdom.

I advise you to thoroughly check out the company you are interested in to ensure that you are choosing wisely. These days, the Internet will help you greatly in this regard. In particular, check with the Direct Selling Association (DSA). If a company is operating illegally, someone will have reported them on the Internet somewhere. However, always cross-check your references, compare comments, and above all, tread wisely.

Myth #2: 95 Percent of Network Marketers Fail

I think the basic flaw with this myth is that it implies that all people who join a company do it for business reasons, and this is not true. People join for their own personal reasons, but they fit into one or more of the following categories:

- ***Customers:*** These are people who have registered with a company to purchase products at either a wholesale or retail price. They are not interested in the business opportunity.

- ***Passive Distributors:*** These are people who join the company as distributors but do not participate in the company. They do not get involved in training programs, they do not interact with their upline or top achievers, they do not go to events, and they do not follow even the basic business-building guidelines. Simply, they do not do anything after they sign on.

- ***Active Distributors:*** These are people who join a company and get into action. They get involved with training, go to events and meetings, ask questions of the top achievers and their upline, read recommended personal development books, and actively build relationships with other distributors. They are fully engaged in building their team and their business, and their intention is to build their business. I have been an active distributor from the get-go.

If it is to be, it is up to me!

Now that we understand that there are three basic categories of people who join a company, let's look into the meaning of the word *fail*. Defining failure is a hard thing to do, because it depends on what you were trying to do in the first place. A famous saying is that you only fail when you stop trying. So if we bring this into consideration as well, it means we have to know if the distributor has thrown in the towel or is simply taking a break and regrouping. I think Steve Mitchell defines it well:

An Active Distributor who followed all their company and field leadership systems, got trained correctly, took all the necessary actions to achieve their goals, but then ultimately gave up and quit on the MLM business completely—which I think is fair criteria to judge if someone is "active" and yet "failed" in MLM.

—Steve Mitchell

Just a word of warning: you are unique, and your dreams, your personal situation, your commitment, your drive, and your hunger are yours. These last three play an enormous part in your level of success. You can't expect to be rewarded if you don't put in the work and the dedication. It is doubtful that you will ever know exactly why some of the active distributors failed, but you do know about your own work ethic and drive to succeed, and if they are strong you could well succeed where others have failed.

When I was competing in hairstyling competitions, I knew we were all qualified, we were all excited about competing, and we were all creative, but the winners had that winning edge, which I learned early on comes from within. Winners want it more than the rest, and they are willing to work harder and longer than the rest to get to the winner's circle.

For many years, I poured my energy into hairstyling competitions and building my hair salon, but it just wasn't enough. We could never get ahead no matter how hungry I was. One evening, I listened to a presenter at a network marketing event, and I instantly knew I could do this. I finally had something I was passionate about that would reward me for my drive and hunger to grow and become free.

I desperately wanted to make a difference in my life and that of my family. I knew what I wanted: freedom to live a life that allowed me to sleep at night; pay my bills; buy my children shoes, clothes, vacations, and extras without depending on a credit card with high interest—in today's terms it all seems so small, but until I found network marketing, I may as well have been trying to get to the moon.

I believe in this industry and profession with all my heart, and I can tell you from personal experience that it is hard to fail if you are clear on why you are doing this. You need to know exactly what it is you want, whether it's to get out of your credit card debt, buy some new clothes for the kids, or become a millionaire. Write it down, and remind yourself daily; believe me, it will help to keep you on track. Set your sights on your dreams, work on your personal development, ask questions of your upline and the top achievers, show up at the events, be persistent, and build those all-important relationships, remembering to give first.

In conclusion, if we are looking to see what percentage are successful in network marketing and whether there is any truth in the idea that 95 percent fail, the only people we can truly look at are the Active Distributors. This is the only group who are actively building their business with the intention of success. The other two categories cannot fail at something they are not even trying to achieve. It is a bit like saying I failed at tennis when all I did was buy a racket but never stepped onto a court; how can I fail at something I never started?

It is important to understand that this is a *business*, and there is always a chance of failure. Network marketing is no different from any other form of business. Some of us will be outrageously successful, some will be moderately successful, and some will close up shop, never to return.

Recent federal government statistics report that approximately 25 percent of small businesses fail in the first year, 36 percent by the end of the second year, and 50 percent by the end of years four and five. These figures apply to all industries across all states, so they could also easily apply to our industry.

When I was researching the government general business failure rates, I came across a table of the main reasons why businesses fail. The list is very interesting, because a number of the reasons why they fail do not necessarily apply to us. For the most part, provided that the company you are working with or researching is reputable and credible, you won't have to concern yourself with the following reasons for failure, because the company has teams of professionals to handle these back-office issues for you:

- having enough inventory
- knowledge of best pricing practices
- emotional pricing
- knowledge about suppliers
- advertising budgets
- business finance
- expanding too rapidly
- lack of planning
- poor credit evaluation of buyers
- experience and knowledge of product or service

There are some points that you *do* have to concern yourself with:

- incompetence
- being compliant and not making outrageous claims that could hurt the company
- living too high for the business—at first it is better to invest your earned money back into the business instead of using it too soon to raise your standard of living
- nonpayment of taxes
- lack of planning

- no experience in record keeping
- neglect
- keeping up to date on product knowledge

Sometimes we make mistakes. The owner of the second company I joined made a claim that ultimately caused the government to close it down. They had a great tax product, and many people were devastated by the final outcome, not the least of which was that the owner ended up in jail. The collapse caused all of us considerable hurt and embarrassment, but we didn't stop. We continued to meet as a team and set about looking for our next networking home.

More Myths About Network Marketing

You Can Quickly Become a Millionaire

This is a profession and not an overnight path to success and riches. There is no magic pill. It takes work, dedication, money, and a willingness to learn, to grow personally, and to risk making mistakes.

The great aspect about becoming a network marketing professional is that you can start your career and business from any station in life. Not everyone is going to the top; not everyone is going to become a millionaire. However, you will increase your chances of reaching your dreams when you get involved and work passionately and persistently.

You Have to Be a Person Who is Good at Selling

This is one of the main reasons why I wrote this book. The Heartfelt Network Marketing philosophy is an alternative to the hard-sell route to the top. You don't have to be a sales person when you follow your heart. This is your own business, and you get to choose your own goals and your own way.

Network Marketing Is a High-Pressure Career

You are your own boss and you set your own schedule and goals. Unlike working for a company as an employee, where you have managers and supervisors telling you what and when to do things, you set your own schedule, and the commute is awesome...usually just down the hall.

By the end of 2014, I had 130,000-plus members in my downline, and surprisingly I personally recruited only 300 and work closely with 5 to 6 at a time. I had recruited 30 people in my very first two weeks. Using people leverage is the way to do this. I work with fewer people in a day than the average mother.

Network Marketing Is Not a Profession

Network marketing is a profession. It requires education, dedication, product knowledge, people skills, presentation skills, and personal development. When people ask me what I do for a living, I say with a great deal of pride that I am network marketing professional. I then pause and say that I absolutely love it. I originally heard one of my greatest mentors, Carole Taylor, use this phrase, and it is so true that I have been using it ever since. My career has provided me with a life that is brighter than any of my early dreams and has allowed me to directly and indirectly change the lives of tens of thousands of people. Thanks to my profession, I am able to say that I have literally saved at least two lives. Why wouldn't I stand tall and be proud of my profession?

Don't let social stigma and ill-informed, preprogrammed stereotype ideas cloud your judgment. Years ago, I let a girlfriend run my life, and it wasn't until she passed away that I realized I had stopped taking responsibility for my own life. I know she believed she was doing the right thing by me, and I know for certain that had she still been alive when I discovered network marketing, she would have strongly discouraged me from becoming a member of this honorable profession.

These are *your* life and *your* dreams. Here is a story that says it all.

A flea can jump very high indeed. However, when left in a jar with the lid on, fleas quickly learn that they can only jump as high as the lid on the jar. When they were let out of the jar, they never jumped any higher than the lid ever again.

Don't let people or your perception of status put you in a jar.

This Is a Heartfelt, Honorable Profession

You beat 50 percent of the people in America by working hard. You beat another 40 percent by being a person of honesty and integrity and standing for something. The last 10 percent is a dogfight in the free enterprise system.

—Art Williams, All You Can Do Is All You Can Do

Let's Start with Honor

I am a professional Heartfelt Network Marketer, and I am proud of it. I believe in my profession and I don't hide it. Why would I? I help people realize their dreams, pay the bills, feed their children, take family vacations, grow personally, create a legacy for their families, and escape financial chains. Oh, and did I mention we create millionaires? I am on a crusade to help people dream and grow into their dreams.

I believe in leading with our heart and head working as one unit. Heartfelt network marketers genuinely care about others and are respectful of their hopes and dreams. I don't believe in selling, though I spent many years doing exactly that. There are times when I have said to a friend or a prospect, "Just give me your social and I will get you going."

Over the years, my beliefs about network marketing and what it takes to be a professional network marketer have evolved. In the beginning, I was taught that it was a numbers game, where the objective was to sell the product or service to the prospect regardless of his or her needs. I was trained to focus on my need to sell and recruit. It was always about volume.

I followed this approach for a few years and always found it difficult, but some top achievers with their wonderful lifestyles advocated this approach and were proof that it worked.

At the start, I was so excited about network marketing that I jumped in and did what I was told pretty much without question. Every now and then, I felt uncomfortable in my gut, but I pushed through it and put it aside. I was too excited to be concerned about building relationships. I just wanted to tell the world about this wonderful way to build a financial future quickly. In my excitement, I didn't stop to ask my prospect what he or she wanted or get to know who he or she was. I didn't care. I could see my future and I just knew my prospect needed what I had to sell.

I was so excited that I literally drowned prospects in information at my first contact. I wanted to make sure they knew everything just in case I didn't get to speak with them again. I didn't want them to miss out on this great opportunity. If you are already in network marketing, you probably know what I am talking about. Looking back, I think a lot of people signed up with me because of my enthusiasm for the business or because it was the only way they were going to get rid of me. At the time, I didn't feel good about it, but I didn't know any better.

I never noticed their eyes glazing over as I continued to speak.

In hindsight, it seems obvious that I made every mistake possible. However, I kept asking questions of people above me, reading personal development books, going to company events, and building my team, until one day I broke through the cloud.

Eventually, I started to meet a wider group of top achievers who had a more genuine approach to network marketing. Coupled with the personal development I was going through, this helped me become more comfortable with my own instincts. I started to see my role as a heartfelt network marketer, where relationships and responding to the other person's needs were paramount. I noticed that by concentrating on these core issues, the numbers took care of themselves.

One of the key lessons I have learned is that

I should treat people the way I like to be treated.

I constantly put myself in the other person's shoes, but I don't stay there too long. Sometimes too much empathy can incapacitate you. Try to see the world through the other person's eyes for a minute. This will help you to open up channels of communication.

It took me many years of personal growth and trial and error to become a Heartfelt Network Marketing professional. Once I realized I needed to concentrate on how best I could help people to dream and give them hope, it only took a few short years to reach my dream life.

The great thing is now that I am here I have a whole new set of dreams, including a dream to be able to help you and thousands of others to reach your dreams.

Years of experience in life and network marketing have culminated in my Heartfelt Network Marketing philosophy. It is built on the traditional network marketing business of building teams and moving products and services, but the emphasis is on needs and dreams, rather than recruitment numbers and sale units.

I have developed an approach and a set of core values based on caring and helping people to believe in themselves and build their dreams. I help them recognize where they are in their lives and the options that are available to them in the future. I focus on their needs.

For the past thirteen years, my belief has been that my product must be of benefit to my prospect and enhance his or her life before I talk about it at any length. I deliberately work at not selling. I am a problem solver, not a sales person.

It starts with your mind-set and your attitude—you have to own Heartfelt Network Marketing and be proud of your network marketing career. You become a great deal more credible when you believe in yourself, your role, your company, and your products and services.

Integrity

If success is not on your own terms, if it looks good to the world but does not feel good in your soul, it is not success at all.

—*Anna Quindlen*

Integrity is a key component of our honorable profession. Living as a person of integrity means that at all times we listen to our heart and our gut instincts and do the right thing according to our personal code of ethics. We are never at a crossroads wondering what to do because the right path is always well lit. Our friends, colleagues, and customers know us to be trustworthy, dependable, and accountable for our actions.

Integrity promotes trust, and this is the basis for a mutually rewarding relationship. People will use the words *trust* and *trustworthy* when talking to their friends about you. Your reputation for being a person of integrity will spread far and wide and is of more value to you than any other asset. Your reputation will open doors and provide unlimited opportunities for you to help people to grow and in the process grow your own business.

Maintaining your reputation for integrity is a lifelong endeavor that is worthy of the price, whatever it is.

In looking for people to hire, look for three qualities: integrity, intelligence, and energy. And if they don't have the first one, the other two will kill you.

—*Warren Buffett, CEO, Berkshire Hathaway*

Trust is paramount when dealing with people, particularly in slow economic times and in any instance that involves their finances. Think about your personal dealings with people in the past. Have you dealt with people you didn't trust? I know that I only deal with people I believe are honest and trustworthy. Let people get to know you and see for themselves that you are an honorable person with integrity. It's not something you tell them—it is who you are.

Your integrity is substantiated by your code of ethics. The following is a list of some of the key elements in my personal code of ethics:

- If it doesn't feel good—don't do it.
- If it is not congruent with my beliefs—don't do it.
- Always answer questions truthfully.

- Treat people in the same manner that I want to be treated.
- Be honest, transparent, and authentic.
- Be genuinely concerned with helping my prospect.
- Do not have a hidden agenda.
- Be open and believable.

You Are Creating a Lifetime Relationship, Not Just Passing Through

The first step in Heartfelt Network Marketing is developing a rapport with your prospect and creating a relationship of mutual respect. You are not interested in a one-off transaction. Focus on developing mutually beneficial lifetime relationships. Not everyone will become a team member or a customer, but if they like you and admire your integrity and professionalism, they may become an advocate and introduce you to a whole new network of people.

The traditional sales methodology is centered on the numbers game and closing ratio. Your closing ratio tells you how many sales pitches you need to make to secure a sale. There is no doubt this works, and I have seen sales people push through all kinds of barriers in the belief that each no is one step closer to a yes. Heartfelt Network Marketing does not work on the numbers game principle and does not require you to learn the twenty most effective closes or the top ten ways to get an appointment.

You work on building a relationship with your prospect so that you can understand what his or her needs and dreams are.

Building a relationship is a two-way street.

You allow your prospect to get to know you as you get to know him or her. Creating an open and friendly communication channel allows both parties to feel relaxed and more open and honest with each other. There is no hidden agenda lurking behind the scenes.

Sometimes a relationship is instant and on other occasions it may take time. Each situation is unique.

You are in the business of growing your business, but this should not come at the expense of your integrity or your prospect. There will come a time in the conversation when you will start to understand what is important to your prospect. If you believe that you have a solution that will work for this person, always ask permission to present your information for consideration. On the other hand, if you know that there is nothing you can do for your prospect, say so. Your honesty will ensure her respect and she will more than likely introduce you to some of her friends who might be a better fit.

The Heartfelt Network Marketing method reduces your chance of rejection because you are not trying to manipulate your prospect, or trying to sell him something he doesn't need. You are only introducing your solution if you believe it will do the job for him.

Relationship selling is a win/win for you and your prospect.

If, after careful fact-finding and analysis, your product or service truly meets your prospect's needs, both parties benefit as a result of the transaction. Building mutually rewarding relationships with people you meet is a way of conducting yourself in business as a person of integrity. You are known to be a professional, ethical, and caring individual, one who is committed to a win/win outcome for all concerned. People will be very comfortable about recommending you to their friends and colleagues. Think about the type of people you recommend to your friends and why.

I urge you to engage in active listening.

When your prospect is talking, honor her by listening to what she is saying rather than anxiously waiting to interrupt with what you want to say next. When your prospect sees that you are really listening to her, she will most likely feel understood.

Status Is a State of Mind

I have met many newbie network marketers who are embarrassed to tell their friends and family what they are doing. They feel that people see them as just above snake oil salesmen. If I felt like that, I wouldn't want to tell anyone either.

People's opinion of you is heavily influenced by how you see yourself. Status starts with your own mind-set and attitude.

If you believe that you are a professional, ethical person with a product or service that you use yourself and genuinely believe in, you will automatically come across as someone worth talking to. Present yourself as a quietly confident, self-assured person with self-respect who treats others in the same manner as you expect to be treated. This is vastly different from someone who is ashamed of what they do and does not genuinely believe in their company or the products and services represented. If you don't believe, why should someone you have just met or a loved one believe you?

We respond to people's own beliefs about themselves.

Stand in front of a mirror and take a good, hard look at yourself. Would you believe this person? Would you do business with this person? Would you introduce this person to your friends and family? Would you feel good about being associated with this person? If you did not answer with a resounding yes on every point, you need to work out why not and put some time and effort into developing the missing beliefs and the physical representation of those beliefs. What I mean by physical representation is your outward appearance. If you respect yourself, your client, and the rules of engagement when it comes to business, you will make an effort to play by those rules to the best of your ability and look like the professional you want to become.

A traditional sales job is vastly different from that of a heartfelt network marketer. You are a self-employed business owner who specializes in introducing your products and services to people who have expressed a need for them. You are a relationship builder who actively listens to what someone needs, and if your product or service can help that person, you ask permission to tell your story, and leave it to the prospect to decide.

You do not manipulate, strong-arm, persuade, or otherwise trick prospects into taking you up on your offer. You do not report to a sales manager or focus on annual targets set by a remote VP of sales. You are your own person with the freedom to focus on creating long-term business relationships, which over time could develop into a substantial business.

At last count, my network marketing business operates in three countries and is over 130,000 strong.

Beware of Ill-Informed Advisors

I realized very early on that the people who were telling me not to enter the network marketing profession were not going to pay my bills, and they knew very little about network marketing. I eventually realized that I was prejudiced about network marketing at the outset without knowing anything about it. It wasn't until I took the time to look into it that I developed a new attitude and became open to learning about network marketing.

Would you take advice on how to become financially free from someone who is drowning in debt? Does it make sense to you to follow someone's recommendations on how to swing a golf club simply because they read a book on how it's done? Surely, it makes a lot more sense to listen to and follow people who are doing what you are considering doing and are going and growing to where you want to be in life.

Network marketing is here to stay, and it continues to grow and become more mainstream as we consumers become more comfortable with the quality and reliability of the industry. Life is hectic and money is tight, so we are looking for quality at a lower cost and the convenience of buying 24-7 with home delivery. We are also buying products based on reviews of people we don't even know and recommendations from our friends because we can't afford to make a mistake with our purchases. We trust a stranger's review more than a multimillion-dollar multimedia advertising campaign. Network marketing companies fit very well with this emerging consumer environment.

The growth of our industry is further guaranteed by the involvement of some of the richest mainstream business people in the world: Warren Buffett, Donald Trump, and Sir Richard Branson are all involved with network marketing, and highly respected authors and commentators on personal finance like Robert Kiyosaki are huge advocates.

If you or someone you respect has a negative perception of network marketing as a business or a career, consider going to a couple of meetings and personally researching it for yourself. This is a great place to start your research into making a well-informed decision.

We Are Heartfelt

Heartfelt means that you genuinely want to make a positive difference in people's lives and give them the benefit of the lessons you have learned.

Sharing your stories and allowing them to see how far you have grown gives them hope and the heart to dream again.

We are real, everyday people who have done what most people believe is impossible.

The point is that we did it using a tried and true process. The things that make the difference between our individual degrees of success are our personal hunger and how hard we are willing to work to realize our dreams. This is where the chapters covering dreams, beliefs, and personal development will help to add fuel to your fire.

We often talk about the trappings of material things like homes, cars, and travel, but over the years I have been rewarded with far more than just money. Thanks to my network marketing business, I was able to help my oldest son make a full recovery from his drug addiction. I was in a financial position to pay for him to stay in a rehabilitation center for several months until he had truly recovered.

I introduced a dear friend to the products manufactured by my current company, and six months later I received a wonderful letter from his son thanking me for saving his father's life. Countless families have been able to pay for their children's college educations, giving them a debt-free start in life.

Other families have been able to get through devastating medical crises without a lifetime of ongoing debt. Average, everyday families have become millionaires and changed their family future for generations to come.

I was able to buy my elderly mother a home and pay for my youngest son's college education. It feels wonderful knowing that my mother wakes up happy everyday living in her beautiful home and that my youngest son is not tied down with years of student loan debt.

This all came from the heart and a passion to show people that it can be done. You can hope and you can dream and you can make it so.

You will get all you want in life if you help enough other people get what they want.

—Zig Ziglar

Heartfelt is also about helping people feel good about themselves. It is our heartfelt responsibility to help people believe in themselves, and quite often all it takes is for someone to say they believe in us. It is amazing how we respond to people's opinions and expectations. It seems that we naturally try to meet people's expectations of us. You can easily lift other people when you acknowledge them and tell them that you believe in them.

I was helping people feel better about themselves long before I started network marketing. In the hair salon, I would do head to toe makeovers, and I loved the excitement in seeing my clients' eyes light up when they realized how really beautiful they could be.

It is common for others to believe in us more than we do ourselves. How many times have your friends and family pointed out your positive characteristics and attributes in the face of your own character assassination?

You don't want to waste the next twenty, thirty, or forty years, as some of us have. I started my part-time network marketing career in my forties, and Jimmy Smith didn't start until he was in his late fifties. However, both of us are now living the life we designed.

I can't guarantee that you will meet your expectations, but I can assure you that the weeks will turn into months and the months into years regardless of whether you go for your dreams or not. Time is out of control, so get going now.

This Is a Profession

To become a professional network marketer requires an ongoing commitment to personal growth and the understanding that you are a business owner. Starting a network marketing career is similar to any other profession, such as accounting or engineering. You establish a four-year study plan and get going. The main difference with network marketing is that you earn while you learn.

Over the years, I have watched people come and go, and the ones who have a clear objective in mind usually take four to five years and maybe more than one networking company before they are truly comfortable in their new career. However, by this time they can be on fire and the next couple of years their growth is exponential. I have also seen people rise to top levels in a much shorter period of time.

This is not just another job. You are building a business and a future. You are building your own retirement fund and creating a financial legacy for your family. It can take time to get the ball rolling, but then thanks to the compound effect of your team growth, it could eventually take on a life of its own.

This is a profession, and to ensure that you are always at the forefront you must allocate time for continual personal growth. I enjoy listening to CDs in the car, and I have made my car my rolling network marketing university.

If you have a regular job, I strongly recommend that you keep it while you are developing your network marketing career and business. A longtime mentor of mine, Stan Barker, suggests that you should have at least eighteen months of income saved up before you transition from part-time to full-time professional network marketer.

Professionals Know and Believe in Their Products, Services, and Compensation Plans

This is your business; the more you know about your products and services and how your compensation plan works, the more quickly you will be able to help others and grow your business.

Use the company tools and literature to speed up your learning process.

Where appropriate, try the products out for yourself. Nothing speaks louder than personal experience.

Keep up to date with your company's product development. They are pouring hundreds of thousands of dollars into ongoing product research and marketing materials, so take advantage of it.

Focus on what your prospects need. Look for the needs and problems that your product or service can deliver on. When your prospects see that you genuinely care about what they want and need, they will feel confident that they are making the right decision in buying from you or joining your team.

Network Marketing Is a Team Sport

We are a professional team and we support and encourage each other, but we take personal responsibility for our successes and failures. Our intention is to not leave people out in the cold; however, because it is a voluntary army, it is up to the individual to decide his or her own pace. Make every effort to introduce people to other like-minded people. The more connected everyone feels, the more energy you have going forward in the same direction.

Mixing and meeting inspired people who have a common interest with you is uplifting in itself.

> *I never miss a major company event, and when I am there I play fully and meet as many people as possible.*

Sleeping is left for the flight home. I am always on the hunt to learn more, and the best way to do this is to speak with the other top achievers and company executives.

In network marketing, you are a playing coach. You are coaching your team members, while your upline is coaching you. At events and three-way calls, I will introduce my team members to the top achievers and company executives. Keeping track of your team members' progress and their level of activity will help to keep them on track.

Do You Want Financial Freedom?

You deserve a chance at having a secondary income stream. If you don't have spare money to invest in a secondary income stream, why not look at building one?

Develop your second income stream while working your day job. Don't jeopardize what you already have by throwing away your regular job before you are generating a solid income stream from your network marketing business.

A few years ago, an extra four hundred dollars a month was considered to be the amount that would have saved about 75 percent of bankruptcies in this country. Now, that amount is probably higher these days, but, even so, just that little extra amount is so doable. Think about taking that four hundred dollars and investing it in something that earns a decent rate of return. It becomes much more than four hundred a month. Or use it for the private school that you currently can't afford to put your kids in…or whatever it is that you dream about. It takes the pressure off if both parties can contribute to the family bank account, especially if one has a job that allows for flexible hours and time to care for the children.

A little extra income could possibly save marriages, because it means fewer arguments about money. Maybe it will help the children feel more settled at school because they have the same clothes and equipment as their peers. Or you can hire tutors to help your children if they can't keep up at school.

Your child's future could be much brighter because you had an extra $100 a month to pay for a tutor.

Deliver on Expectations

Another way to build trust is to keep your word. From follow-up calls to delivering on time, keeping your word is one of your most powerful sales tools. Of course, unexpected things do happen, and sometimes you cannot keep your promises. When this occurs, communicate with your prospect or customer and inquire as to whether the change is workable and what you can do to lessen the inconvenience. That way, you keep your trust level intact, or you may even strengthen it as a result.

Your professionalism is defined not by the business you are in but by the way you are in business.

—*Tony Alessandra*

Follow up with your new clients and team members. This is the time to find out how your client likes your product or service and, more importantly, uncover any concerns he or she may have. It is also a great time to make sure that your new recruit understands the compensation plan and any milestones that may be coming up that might help him or her to progress.

Often people won't call you to complain, but they will complain to everyone they meet. You need to know about this as soon as possible so that you can fix the problem and turn a potential disgruntled customer into a fan.

Following up regularly provides an ideal opportunity to create repeat business and get referrals for new prospects. When was the last time a person who sold you a product or provided a service called you to see how everything was going? How did you feel about it?

Build a Family Business—No Prior Experience Necessary

Build your business by leveraging your network marketing company. They have done the groundbreaking work for you and created a solid business base for you to build on. The company provides you with what you need:

- Systems
- Products and services
- Ongoing research
- Marketing materials
- Training
- Sales tools
- References
- Websites
- Testimonials
- Role models
- Financial incentives
- Support network
- Marketing intelligence
- Connections
- Brand recognition
- Back-office administration
- Payroll
- Debt collecting
- Board of directors
- Business specialists
- A dream and a revenue stream

In short, the company provides everything you need to grow a multimillion-dollar business, and your task is to grow the business.

Just before I started my network marketing career, I read *The E-Myth* by Michael Gerber, and I learned that running my own regular business meant I had to be everyone from the CEO to the janitor. I just wanted to be the creative hair stylist and the customer service person, but I had to keep multitasking until the day I closed my hair salon.

Since the day I transitioned to a full-time professional network marketer, I have been able to concentrate on the aspects I love about my career. I get to travel, meet people, create rewarding relationships, and help people with their hopes and dreams.

This business allows you to learn on the job and get paid while you are doing it. A college degree is not required; however a thirst for personal growth, a great work ethic, and a passion for paying it forward are necessary if you want to be one of the top achievers.

You Own Your Networking Business

A network marketing business is your business. You are the CEO, and you make all the rules regarding your level of commitment and your performance targets. You are responsible for what, where, how, and when you work.

It is your responsibility to meet your own expectations and to do whatever is necessary to meet those targets; remember you are not alone. You have access to an unlimited support network: role models, advisors, mentors, business colleagues, and training programs all specializing in your business. You also have a team of like-minded business owners helping to grow your business even when you are on vacation or asleep. I have business owners in places as far away as Australia working on the business when I am sleeping. Recently, my husband Scott and I took an impromptu seven-week vacation overseas, and the business continued to grow without missing a beat.

This truly is a career where you get paid what you deserve. There is generally no ceiling to how much you can earn or how large you can build your business.

You can also turn your network marketing career into a family business. I enrolled my three children into my current company, and I know several top achievers who have created multiple generations of millionaires in the latter part of their lifetime. Jimmy Smith is a great example of this. Jimmy's legacy to his family will live on for generations to come.

In many companies, your network marketing business is salable or willable.

Easy Global Expansion and Free Support

Technology has truly created a global village. You can connect with people on the other side of the world just as quickly and easily as your next-door neighbor.

Most networking companies are international, which means you can grow your business globally. This is particularly great for those of you with friends and relatives living in different countries or friends and neighbors who have overseas connections.

Unlike in a traditional business, where setting up an overseas branch of your business would take an enormous amount of research, time, and money, you can open your overseas networking business within minutes. All you need is a relationship with someone living in the country or area you want to expand into or a person who knows a person in that area.

Prior to opening up in another country, you should check with your corporate headquarters to find out exactly what is required and how your foreign business will operate. My business has expanded into Australia and China, and I did this while on vacation in these countries.

Running your overseas team can be both exciting and challenging, but it is definitely doable and rewarding, because your company freely provides all of the necessary business training and support functions including back-office administration, online training, product/service distribution, customer support, and sales management.

You Decide When and How You Retire

Network marketing can help your retirement in many different ways. Firstly, you can start your network marketing business even in retirement, and it is your choice when to retire from your network marketing career, if ever.

At sixty, it is probably too late to go back to college, get a degree, and start a new income-producing career, but you can start building a networking business a few nights a week and three or four hours on a Saturday. It takes time to build up your networking business, but unlike a university degree, you will be earning an income from the get-go and not starting at ground zero after four years of study. I know of many people who in five or six years have been able to quit their day jobs and be financially self-sufficient.

Retirement is supposed to be the time in your life when you are your own boss and can go and do what you please. Unfortunately, due to the economy or life itself, many people reach retirement with a minimal personal pension or they are completely dependent upon the government. Either option makes for a pretty dismal and sad retirement.

Starting a network marketing career or maintaining it as you approach retirement will help your retirement planning.

You will be building an income stream similar to a pension, except that this business has the potential to keep growing. A lot of people have recently lost their retirement funds or they have been severely reduced due to the economic upheaval. If you're sixty and you have a day job, your 401(k) may no longer be enough to keep you going, and working harder or longer hours at your day job is not going to make a great deal of difference. Whereas starting to grow a residual income part time will add to your ability to survive and thrive in your retirement.

Personal Development

Personal development is the belief that you are worth the effort, time, and energy needed to develop yourself.

—Denis Waitley

Personal development is the cornerstone of Heartfelt Network Marketing, and encompasses your character, skill set, knowledge base, relationships, finances, lifestyle, and dreams. The great aspect of personal growth is that it is a lifetime adventure you can start anywhere, any time, and at any age.

The one thing I can guarantee you is that if you are not growing you are going backward.

I started my lifelong love affair with personal development when I was a young mother. I attended a six-week parenting class seven times because I was a teenage mom and I wanted to learn how to be a great mom. From the time I started my own hair salon, I would often tell my hair salon clients about some amazing lesson I had just learned from my latest book on psychology or motivation. Sometimes I was so passionate about the book I would buy copies and give them to my clients as gifts, which is a practice I still do today with my friends, family, and team members.

Signing up for network marketing is signing up for personal development. I have learned so much more about myself, business, relationships, and the world than I ever would have working alone in my private studio hair salon. The more I grow, the more I do different things, dream different dreams, and see further.

Personal development is a positive upward spiral: the more you participate in personal growth, the more you want to do it, and the more you benefit from doing it. There is no downside.

Personal development often starts with people of low self-esteem, so if this is where you are, get off the bench and get into the game. Develop a desire and passion to grow, learn, and expand your horizons. Care enough about yourself and those around you, especially your children, to grow. Become your children's role model and start a generational upswing that will last for generations.

Follow an intentional growth plan matched to your dream. There's no point in learning French if you are moving to Japan.

If you are new to network marketing and not sure if it is for you, I strongly recommend that you start your personal growth adventure, even if you don't become a professional network marketer. Remember, there is no downside to working on yourself.

Everything you learn while developing and working your Heartfelt Network Marketing career will help every aspect of your life.

Your Growing Business

Your Continuous Personal Growth

Your Lifestyle Will Grow as You Grow

To grow, you are required to move outside of your comfort zone from time to time, including investing time, money, and extra effort in your personal development. Everything comes with a price, and in this case, I like to think of it as an investment in your future.

Before things can change, you must change. Before things can grow, you must grow.

You may also have to buy new clothes, go to state and national events, purchase personal development books, and attend courses and seminars—all of these things will cost you time and money, but look to your future because that is where you are headed.

The price is sometimes time—time for team calls, to study, and to travel to events, along with time away from your family.

Look at your entry into network marketing in the same way that you would think of studying part time for a degree while holding down your full-time job. The key difference here is that network marketing allows you to earn as you learn while maintaining your day job.

I noticed that as I was growing in character and ability, my checks were growing as well. I was getting paid to do things I wanted to do with my life—become a better mom, a better wife, a better friend, and a better businessperson.

I was inspired by my mentors and colleagues to learn more about what I could do with my life. I was learning to really look at my life, and I started to understand that there was nothing wrong with money. There is nothing wrong with having a newer car or a newer house assuming you can pay for it.

I started to dream and follow my plan, and then the next thing I knew I was looking at buying a home.

I remember driving into the neighborhood and getting the idea that I could really buy a house. I didn't have to live in that little apartment that had served its purpose when I was starting out. On the day that I actually signed the contract for my house, I think I drove through that neighborhood ten times. I'd drive through the neighborhood one way, and then I'd come in the other way, and then I'd drive through the middle. I would pass by the house slowly and think, *That's my house.*

I picked up the keys from the real estate agent before the contracts were processed and let myself in. They had left behind a desk chair. I scooted it up to the window and just sat there reveling in the thought that I was a single mom and a homeowner due to my network marketing income. I was thinking, *I have a house for my son and a garage to drive into at night that doesn't scare me.* The apartment behind my salon didn't have a garage, so I had to park in the city parking lot down the street. The street level door didn't have a lock, so sometimes vagrants or drunks would wander up there to use the restroom. Then it was a mad dash up the twenty-eight creaky stairs to my three-room apartment. Back then, I think the garage was even more important than the house.

There is no better feeling than reaching for a dream and succeeding. I relive the wonderful feelings I felt the day I sat alone looking out the window of my new home time and time again.

I get so excited when somebody comes to a meeting and I see that they have that little spark in their eyes. I know the journey they are on. I know that if they stay the course, one day they will achieve their dreams and feel the feelings I feel every time I reach a new milestone.

Your network marketing business will only grow as big and as quickly as you do, so get going.

Time's a wastin'.

What Are Your Natural Strengths and Talents?

Plan your personal development to match your dreams and your natural abilities.

Make your strengths productive and your weaknesses irrelevant.

Don't spend unnecessary time on your weaknesses. Invest that time in working on your strengths. If you are not sure what they are, ask the people who are closest to you. They will very quickly set you right.

Align your talents with your dreams and build your strengths.

—Anonymous.

I heard this incredible bit of wisdom at a network marketing meeting, and knowing this one thing set me free. I had been so worried about all the things I was not good at that I thought it would take years to get going, but after hearing that I should forget about all of that and concentrate on what I could do, I felt empowered. I knew I didn't have to spend years working on the skills I didn't have and I could start building my new career. All I had to do was align my dreams with the skills I had and go fast.

Joni and I both worked in a people business. I was a hairdresser and she owned a women's weight-loss center, so the two things we were very good at were listening and talking. It turns out that these are pretty good skills for network marketing. When Joni and I started out, she was a natural closer and I was a born opener. It was not unusual for us to work together, utilizing our respective talents when appropriate, and we had so much fun working together.

Personal Development and Money

Originally, I dreamed of having the freedom to make my own choices and pay some bills—certainly not to become a millionaire. Financial independence was a by-product of my personal growth and the hard work I put into escaping the four walls of my hair salon.

After you become a millionaire, you can give all of your money away, because what's important is not the million dollars; what's important is the person you have become in the process of becoming a millionaire.

—Jim Rohn

Your dreams may not include becoming a millionaire either, and that is perfectly OK. However, obtaining financial freedom or even a small financial boost may help you to get off the credit card spiral and rid yourself of the sadness, pressure, and frustration that goes with it.

Heartfelt Network Marketing is about achieving your dreams through helping other people achieve theirs, which means sooner or later we have to get down to the business side of things. The business is the vital ingredient that turns our hopes and dreams into reality. You need to get comfortable with making money and talking about money. Money is the energy we need to transform lives and help others who cannot help themselves. There's nothing wrong with it, and it is not the most important thing in the world, but as Zig Ziglar says, "It's right up there with oxygen."

It may seem that too much emphasis is placed on money, but you need to realize that once the money part is taken care of, you are free to choose the things that really make a difference in your life.

Developing yourself and your network marketing business is so much more than money, but money gives you options. It provides you with the means to get things done and help your family and friends. I will always feel a deep sadness that prior to my success in network marketing I couldn't help my daughter pay for her college tuition or her wedding. I couldn't even afford to fly to New Orleans to be with her when she went shopping for her wedding dress. I couldn't help with wedding plans, and I wasn't able to attend her wedding shower. I was in Washington working in my salon. It wasn't until I became a professional network marketer that I could afford to help my children with their dreams, and now I am making up for all those wonderful times I missed with my children.

Unless you were born wealthy, most of us start out somewhere between dirt poor and living paycheck to paycheck. It doesn't matter where you are on the financial scale, what matters is that you understand that as you grow, your business, your friends, and your wealth usually grow with you.

I discovered very quickly that the more I grew personally the bigger the checks grew, and the more giving I could be simply because I had more money.

As you grow, include your children in your business, even if they don't understand or believe in it at first. One day they will understand, and your foresight will pay off for them. I enrolled my three children into my current company within weeks of joining because I could see that it would give them an enormous financial boost. They didn't want to know anything about it at the time, and I decided that mother knows best and started building the business with them tucked in place for maybe someday.

Five years later, the day came when my daughter Heidi took over the reins of her network marketing business. She is now well on her way to building her own multimillion-dollar business.

One of my first financial dreams was to have enough money to buy a used car that was in better condition than my old rust bucket. I was so excited the day I picked up my "new old" car that you would have thought I had just won the lottery. Sixteen years later, I drive a Porsche Panamera, which was not something I dreamed about at the start. Just like everything else, your dreams will grow as you grow.

My lifestyle is a direct product of my continual personal growth and passion to help people hope, dream, and achieve.

You Get Paid to Grow

Growing as a person is a reward on its own, but growing and getting paid along the way is great. Network marketing is an industry that has the ability to pay you while you are learning and growing. When you start out you may only get paid one hundred dollars a week, but this beats paying someone one hundred dollars to teach you.

Many people pay out thousands of dollars a year for personal development seminars, coaching, and live events. Others pay thousands for business coaching and sales training. Often you have to work out how to apply their advice to your career and business, because the trainers and speakers are from a variety of industries and backgrounds. There is certainly nothing wrong with spending money on your personal, financial, and business growth, but network marketing provides a way to get more bang for your buck.

Network marketing is overflowing with material, books, speakers, trainers, and managers who specialize in network marketing.

Sometimes you will have to buy a book, or pay to travel to an event. This is an investment, not an expense. The extra great benefit to belonging to a networking company is that often the motivational events are free to members, and you will likely be able to speak to the presenters and authors in person. Even more important than the quality and minimal cost of the training is the opportunity to immediately put into practice what you have learned and start recouping your investment.

Network marketing pays you while you learn and grow, and the more you learn and grow, the more it pays you.

The Ideal Growth Environment

Mix with like-minded people who are also into personal development to supercharge your personal growth. You have made a commitment to changing and taking control of your future, so now is the time to understand how to create the very best conditions for your growth. To become an energized, can-do type of person, you need to be around action-oriented people, so that you can learn from them and have friends and colleagues you can relate to and have fun with.

Like-minded people usually hang out together. This is because we have ideas and thoughts in common and communication is easy. We may not necessarily agree on every point, but we can relate to one another.

Have you ever been in a situation where you had nothing in common with the people around you? It tends to be difficult to get involved in the discussions, and eventually you find yourself slinking to the door to make an escape. It is much more fun and exciting to mix with people who are like-minded, and when it comes to personal development, network marketing delivers in spades.

Personal growth takes time, and there are lessons to be learned and practiced. Create a relationship or an environment where you are not alone. I started my journey with my friend Joni, and then Angela soon joined and we made it a friendly, competitive game. I found that there is no better place than the network marketing industry to nurture personal development. Network marketing is all about personal development, and you will be mixing with people from all different stages in their personal growth. Some people will be just starting out, others will be going through a growth phase, and there will be those who have reached one peak and they are onto the next. There are hundreds of role models and people to talk to. Whenever I didn't know something, I would ask a person I referred to as my wise person how she would handle the situation, what would she recommend I do, or what book should I read. There was always a limitless well of knowledge and experience I could drink from, and no one ever made me feel ignorant or inferior for asking.

Growing is not always easy sailing, and sometimes you will experience growing pains. In network marketing, you will always have someone to talk to who can relate to what you are doing or where you are going.

Being able to celebrate triumphs with people who understand what it took to get there is exhilarating. You just know what they are feeling, and it is contagious.

Network marketing is not like a nine-to-five job. You don't answer to anyone above you, and you don't have to while away your day sitting in a cubicle looking like you are working when you have nothing left to do. You are your own boss, and you work when it suits you. In 2013, I was able to leave on a seven-week vacation to China and Australia at a moment's notice. Being able to do this is empowering, and I get to grow even more when I meet top achievers from other countries.

You are the CEO of your network marketing business, which means you determine what your performance goals are and who you want to work with. You get to create your ideal work environment.

The most exciting and inspiring environment is the company event.

Most networking companies have at least two national events each year, and they are a must. Joni and I would travel together, and we would bring our teams to the events. We had so much fun buying new clothes, and I'd do everyone's hair for evening events. We would share hotel rooms and buy little presents to give to our team. The camaraderie was fantastic, and everyone was excited about life and what we were doing. We would inspire our teams, and they would reward us with their enthusiasm and stories.

Joni, Angela, and I were invited many times to the top leaders' private cocktail hour, where they would encourage and inspire us to grow further, and then we would go back to our hotel room with our teams and pass it on. For the first few years, Joni and I were never flush with money or time; we found the time and we even borrowed the money to go to the events and promote the products. We considered it investing in our business rather than spending money.

> *You cannot miss a big event. They are visual and emotional proof that network marketing works, and you must be there. The incredible people you will meet at these events are life-changing, and you won't meet them anywhere else other than at a network marketing event.*

Events are everything; they instantly renew your belief in yourself and your dream.

Environments You Should Avoid

There are also environments to avoid if possible. It seems that personal development is not something everyone is interested in or willing to know anything about.

The naysayers are usually the ones who follow Chicken Little's belief that the sky is falling; rather than encouraging you to grow they constantly put you down and remind you that you will never get what you want.

I believe that these people want you to stay down with them so that you will maintain the status quo. Misery loves company. It is easier to keep you down with them than to face the guilt and discomfort they would feel if you actually managed to rise above it all and escape.

Look at the people around you. I know you can't just change your family and friends overnight, but maybe you could try adding a few more dreamers and can-do people like you into the mix and reducing the time you spend with the naysayers—just a thought.

You are the average of the five people closest to you.

—Jim Rohn

Ask Questions

Don't wait until everything is just right. It will never be perfect. There will always be challenges, obstacles, and less than perfect conditions. So what? Get started now. With each step you take, you will grow stronger and stronger, more and more skilled, more and more self-confident and more and more successful.

—Mark Victor Hansen

Most of us don't like asking questions for fear of looking silly or ignorant. A networking event is the best time and place to ask questions. Another great time is the meeting after the meeting. You are in a room filled with like-minded people who have been where you are now, and the Heartfelt Network Marketing philosophy is to help each other.

If you are currently not a network marketer, I strongly recommend that you invest some time and money and go to a company event. Prepare a list of the top five or six questions you have about network marketing and go to the event with the intention of meeting as many people as you can to ask them your questions. Introduce yourself honestly as someone who is checking out the company and the industry and then ask if they would kindly help you by answering a few questions. You will be pleasantly surprised how easy it is, and you will meet some great people as well as get your answers. Try it!

If you are already a network marketer and looking to pick up some momentum and get more involved, the best way is also to go to your next company event. Purposefully interact with the group. Ask them how they are doing and ask their opinion on aspects of your business that you would like some input on. Most of us love answering questions about the business and talking about personal development, and you may surprise yourself with the amount of knowledge you already have.

Sometimes it is not until someone asks you a question that you appreciate how knowledgeable you already are.

Ask Your Sponsor and Upline

When you join a networking company, one of the most important sets of questions to ask your upline is what it takes to move up the ranks in the company. Each company is different, but they all come down to reaching a specific sales target in a set period of time.

I have always found that having a target and a time to meet that target is inspiring. You are growing yourself and your business anyway, so why not set up some milestones? It would be terrible if you found out after an important date that you were only a few points away from a key milestone and you missed out simply because you didn't ask your upline for details on upcoming competitions and bonus pools, or you were too busy to look it up yourself.

Your upline and sponsor are not the only resources available. You will meet and form friendships with many other network marketers, and often it is these friends who can and will have the answers.

During the early years of my current company, I wanted to reach a new rank called Four Star Executive, and I was close but not close enough to meeting the deadline. With fourteen hours to go, I called my friend and upline Lisa Iossi. We had met at an event and bonded right away. Lisa was much younger than me and on a different team, but I just knew she would know how to get me over the line.

I called her and explained my situation and asked her for help. Her first words were, "We only have till midnight—let's go for it!

I think I called her every hour during that day, constantly asking questions about our progress and what to do next. Believe it or not, we made it with one minute to go. Without my asking Lisa for help and without Lisa jumping in to battle with me, I never would have made it.

You don't need to be a newbie to ask questions. You aren't expected to know everything about everything, but it does help to know what you don't know and find people who can fill in the gaps.

When it comes to computers, my mind gets a bit cloudy, and I knew that to get over the line I needed to know minute by minute how I was doing during those last ten hours. That required computer savvy. So I knew what I didn't know, and I knew someone who could more than fill the gap. I called Lisa, and she came through, and I am happily forever in her debt.

Asking a Top Achiever

Learning is exciting, and asking questions of people who have a proven track record is the fastest and surest way to advance your business. I know firsthand how daunting it is to approach a top achiever at an event, but you can do it, and you can build a great relationship at the same time.

The first thing you need to do is prove to the person that you are serious about your network marketing career by turning up to events and participating. Achieve milestones and awards and show up at all company events.

There are thousands of people who want to spend time with the top achievers, so you need to stand out from the crowd and make them feel they are helping a rising star join their ranks.

Company events are the place to get noticed by the company owners and top achievers, even if you are not asked to formally walk on stage. Joni and I made up our networking song at our very first major event, and we got noticed for all the right reasons. Our enthusiasm and willingness to play full out from the get-go had people from everywhere coming up to greet us and join our party.

Getting noticed because of your enthusiasm gives you a green light to approach the top achievers, ask them questions, and get to know them better and form a relationship with them.

I was always asking the top achievers how they did this and that. I wouldn't just rush up to them with my list of questions. I would start out with a casual question and slowly build up. If I heard a particular top achiever speak at an event or on a training video and he or she resonated with me, I would say, "I heard you speak recently and I admire the way you…" I would also ask what I could do to thank the person for his or her time.

I remember one presenter in particular who made it look so easy to get up onstage and talk to a roomful of network marketers. His name was Joe, and he came to a meeting looking like one of us—a little more casually dressed than most top achievers. He carried a tablet when he was speaking on stage, and he made a big deal of it, constantly referring to his notes. He'd say, "Oh, I'm sorry, I'm not that polished." He would go back to his notes on his tablet and say, "Oh yes, I wanted to talk about this." It was totally unpolished, and I related to him.

At the end of his presentation, I went up to him and thanked him. I said, "Wow, you make me think that I can do this, because you didn't mind showing us that you used notes." We instantly became friends, and I had another great achiever in my personal support network.

Joni, Angela, and I would ask questions about something we were having difficulties with, and just listening to their answers and the enthusiasm in their voices would get our self-belief engine working overtime. We would try out whatever they told us to do at the very next opportunity. We also followed up with our team and gave them the benefit of the tips we had just learned from a top achiever.

I would ask questions of everybody I wanted to learn from. I'd ask them a whole range of questions. *Where did you come from? What was it like growing up? Why did you do this? Why did you look at this? Why would you do this, when everybody makes fun of it? What did your husband say? How did you get around that? What did your wife say? How does your wife like what you are doing? What do your kids say?* I would find out from every single person why they did what they did. Sometimes the answers would connect with me, and sometimes they wouldn't. Either way was fine, because I had another person's point of view, which I could learn from, and I would learn how to do things better just by asking the questions.

People you connect with make all the difference—they will give you the answers if you ask. The important thing is to show you have a great attitude and willingness to help others in return.

Role Models and Mentors

If you are not in the process of becoming the person you want to be, you are automatically engaged in becoming the person you don't want to be.

—*Dale Carnegie*

Mentors are so important to us at any and every stage of our lives, and I am so fortunate that the mentors I have met during my network marketing career have all been giving of their time; I can call on them when needed; they are natural teachers; they taught me to dream; they fed me on excitement and their stories.

I started out sitting in the audience watching and listening to the top achievers on stage. Just from listening to them I became inspired and hopeful that I could do this and build my dreams on a solid foundation.

When there was a speaker who caught my attention at a deeper level, I would always work out some way to meet him or her and develop a relationship. Some of them became my mentors, and I owe them a great deal. In fact, I am not sure I would have reached my dreams without them. Each one helped me take a step forward.

Mentors are your personal coach. They show you the way and help you to stay on track. They encourage and inspire you to keep going and help reinforce your growing belief in yourself and your dreams. They won't do the work for you—that's your job.

I have many stories about the wonderful mentors I have been fortunate to work with over the years in network marketing. There is no way I would ever have met these incredible people, let alone become friends with them, without network marketing. You just don't get the opportunity to come across these people in everyday life on a regular basis.

At my first events early on, I realized that I was a student and a beginner in this new profession. I was hungry and excited, and my early mentors never knew how much they gave me from the stage.

Early on, I met Tom "Big Al" Schreiter at a generic training event separate from the company training. His message was powerful, and yet it was simple common sense. Through his training, I began to see how I could do this. I had nothing to lose and practiced on everyone. Joni, Angela, and I had so much fun learning our new language, and we practiced on each other. It was kind of like studying for a college exam but way more fun. We knew we passed the test when people followed us.

Looking back, I always had a mentor: a wise person I looked up to for insights into the challenges and experiences he or she had already faced. My mentors had wisdom of the years I didn't have at the time.

I am so grateful for my first mentor in hairdressing, Gene Herrera, who hired me right out of beauty school. He taught me to come in early and stay later than others, to build clientele quickly, go to all the shows, and compete in the hair competitions. Watching and observing him with his clients was invaluable in gaining confidence.

This experience and relationship with a mentor was powerful stuff for a seventeen-year-old girl working and living in an adult world. I had someone I could ask questions to and who could help guide me.

I always worked for people I could look up to and learn from creatively. Four such people I am so grateful for are Sherman Kendall of the House of Sherman Hair Company; Toni Sheracki of Kami Hair in Salt Lake City, Utah; Phil Dore of Dore Dore Salon Louisiana; and most of all, Kaiji of Kaiji Hair Company in Salt Lake City, Utah. I worked with these artists and fell in love with the art of hair.

As a young mom, I sought out wiser, older people with more life experience to help me. One such person was Burt Chamberlain, a child psychologist I met through a parenting class. His advice was just what I was hungry for at the time. Learning from his experiences and stories guided me through those early years. He also taught me to keep a sense of humor above all else. Burt was such a valuable advisor for the most important job of my life, being a mom.

That takes us to fifteen years ago, when I discovered network marketing—a whole new career to experience and grow into.

My first company had many good speakers who inspired me from the stage, but I realized I needed something more: a wise person I could learn from and build a closer relationship with. Being able to see someone you admire and respect in action is priceless. Network marketing gives you that experience. You can see, hear, and learn from the top achievers, and over time you have the chance to develop relationships with some of them.

I never walked up to someone and just started asking questions. I first showed them that I was hungry to make it in the business and committed to my team's success. After they could see I was serious about personal and business growth, they were happy to help me.

My first network marketing mentor was Coby Gibson. Coby helped build a bridge for me and was so believable and helpful. I was a sponge, hungry to learn from him. He had overcome so much and didn't let anyone stop him from growing and succeeding in spite of the odds. I found his energy and wisdom invaluable and still consider his mentorship as one of the major reasons for my staying the course and not quitting. We ended up in our second company working together. Coby had a huge heart to help friends and family, and his sense of humor was contagious. He was a true rags-to-riches story about perseverance.

Fast forward. I met a man who took my belief in myself and network marketing to a whole new level: Stan Barker. His big hugs and loving fatherly way made our weekly meetings something I looked forward to with great anticipation. I wanted to succeed, and through his eyes I began to see that success was inevitable if I stayed the course. Doubting myself was not an option with a mentor like Stan. He started a weekly mastermind and I drove an hour each way to attend. With his mentoring and patience, I was able to see that this elusive business I hadn't quite figured out yet was waiting for me. I learned from Stan some simple but very important parts to this puzzle of network marketing. For example, the most important meeting is the "meeting after the meeting," where relationships really develop. I am talking about just hanging out having coffee or a meal—getting to know one another.

One of my favorite things Stan did was recommend books and CDs that would feed my hunger to grow. One of my favorites is The Magic of Thinking Big by David Schwartz.

Stan was an Amway Diamond years back when they delivered product to his garage; he would have his downline pick it up from him each week. So he really understood the advantage of building relationships and the personal touch. He told me stories of meeting the greats who pioneered before us in Amway and of his and his family's relationships with them. He shared about fun times, inspirational stories, and stories of giving back. He developed a close relationship with Bill Britt, and one of Bill's students, Jim Brooks, became one of Stan's closest friends. Scott and I recently spent time with Jim and his wife Lin before his death after a long struggle with arthritis. Through Stan's introduction, Scott and I are forever grateful to have personally heard Jim's many amazing stories and experiences. Jim is another rags-to-riches story that inspired me not to give up. Jim's CD, titled Free Enterprise was my go-to recording when I needed inspiration. I listened to it over and over again, literally hundreds of times.

Stan, Coby, Patti, Chris, Angela, and I continued to work together in my second company, The Tax People. It closed its doors six months after I joined, and we were all devastated. We loved the company, people, product, energy, and of course the money. But while we were all searching for a new home, Stan suggested we still meet together each week at our usual meeting place and go through the old VHS tapes he had from years back with Dexter and Bill Britt. It was so powerful, and I am so grateful for this education I received from the original greats of the profession.

Stan was and still is a mentor, my wise networking marketing mentor that I look to for advice and wisdom.

Experience is the best teacher.

After several years and a few more network marketing companies, Stan and I eventually got back together in my current company, but together or not, he is and always has been a great teacher to me.

Over the last twelve years, I have enjoyed learning from a great coach and mentor named Carole Taylor. She is so wise, and after listening to a particular problem or concern in her wisdom she says, "I think you have just answered your own question." That's the power of a great mentor. Helping you to grow and recognize you have answers inside; it just takes a good listener to bring them out.

I consider Carole and her husband Peter an example I aspire to follow. Integrity is at the core of her teaching. Through Carole I met another great teacher whom I love and appreciate as well named Jimmy Smith. He became a student of network marketing at the age of fifty-seven, when he was forced to retire due to an injured back from his previous career as a butcher.

He was fascinated with the geometric progression of the numbers. I love listening to him teach. I am so grateful for the twelve-year friendship I've had with Jimmy. I love sharing the valuable lessons learned from his vast array of experiences in network marketing from the seventeen companies he has participated in on his own journey.

That's why I believe so strongly that anyone can do this if they find mentors and don't quit on the way.

Make your strengths productive and your weaknesses irrelevant. Having mentors on your journey along with your own commitment to be a true networking professional will help you stay the course.

You don't need permission to change or grow, you just need the right person to show you how. It is a lot easier to learn by example. I'm not a great cook and it is always easier for me to follow a recipe. It is even better if I can see what it is supposed to look like or watch someone else making the dish. The same goes for personal development—ask and observe others you admire.

Personal development requires both role models and mentors, and there is a great difference between them. A role model is someone you admire and respect and want to emulate. Role models are usually remote and there is very little to no interaction with them at a personal level. You can learn just about everything there is to know about them, but the relationship is one-way. Many times role models do not know you personally; you are learning from them by observation and study.

A mentor is someone who is on the same path as you. He or she is in the same industry or sport or has the same philosophy as you, relating to you at a personal level and providing firsthand practical guidance and interaction. Your mentor is an experienced and trusted advisor who understands your situation and guides you accordingly.

Mentors are ahead of you in their travels, but they are headed in the same direction as you.

The key difference between a role model and a mentor is interaction. A mentor will have meaningful and direct interaction with you, while a role model may be remote and someone you observe.

Role models are great, but nothing beats hands-on interaction with a mentor.

Most of us find our first role models in the media and books. Find someone you admire and respect and read as much about them as possible. You may find that all, or only some, of their characteristics and principals align with you, and either one is OK. It would be amazing to find a role model who supplies all your answers. Model yourself on the qualities that you relate to or want to develop.

Start your search for a role model with books, and then try to find a person you can actually see and, if possible, interact with, albeit on a small scale.

Our network marketing industry is overflowing with people who are passionate about success and growing, and you have ready access to them on a regular basis.

This is one of the reasons why top achievers are so important in our industry—they are accessible role models with the added advantage that they are traveling in the same direction as us.

Role models and mentors are vital; however, team leaders are equally important and knowledgeable. Thanks to network marketing, I have met and now know hundreds of highly motivated, hardworking team leaders. These incredible people are all contributing to my personal and business growth while on their own journey, and vice versa through example.

Don't limit your mentors to those you meet in your networking company. There are many great teachers and resources who will help you grow, and sometimes getting a different perspective on something can be very helpful.

Nicki and Grace Keohohou, owners of the DSWA, are two of my most dear mentors. They have given me so much over the years, and I am very grateful for their wisdom. Their integrity and understanding of the profession and experience, along with their passion for people, has been so inspiring to me. I love learning, and they make it fun and break it down for the beginner as well as the seasoned networker.

Another great source of role models and mentors is a mastermind. Scott and I participate in Art Jonak's annual Mastermind Event, and it has been a great step in our journey. Attending masterminds is a must for leaders to grow. It is also a way for beginners to quickly learn valuable lessons from the experiences of a variety of mentors. We also attend a number of general and Internet networking trainings each year to keep up with the latest trends in communication, social media, and the like.

Mentoring is like the pebble in the pond. I learn from these people, and then I teach and share to a group of people, who then teach Heartfelt Network Marketing. We are privileged to be able to pay it forward.

Growth Resources

Your attitude, not your aptitude, will determine your altitude.

—Zig Ziglar

These days there is an unlimited pool of resources you can tap into. Personally, I have loved reading inspiring books and forming relationships with top achievers who have paved the way for us.

There is a great story by Earl Nightingale called "Field of Diamonds." I apologize to Earl for my paraphrasing, but if you would like to hear the full story, check it out in the references section at the back of the book.

A farmer sells his farm to go in search of diamonds. Years later, poor and destitute, he returns to his old farm to find that the farmer who purchased his farm had become rich. "How?" he asked, and the new farmer explained that the diamonds had been in the field all the time—he just had to look.

Your field of diamonds is your network marketing industry. Diamonds are all around you in the form of mentors, role models, top achievers, books, videos, online training courses, live events, and CDs. You just need to look for them and use them. Earl was referring to the diamonds within us, and that is true too. You are surrounded by diamonds and sometimes other people will see the diamond in you before you do!

Your Sponsor, Upline, and Company

Your best personal resources are your upline, other network marketers, the company's top achievers, and the company-supplied sales and educational tools, so carefully chose the company you join.

If you are not getting the type of support you are seeking from your upline, you can call the company and ask them to suggest the closest upline who would be willing to help you grow and move up quickly through the ranks. Of course, it is ultimately up to you.

Meet with your upline and work out a growth plan for yourself. Include a strategy, milestones, and goals, and then work it. Commit to the plan and your upline.

Your upline and the top company achievers want to help. They won't do the work for you, but they provide great advice and support.

I remember when Jimmy Smith agreed to be the guest speaker at one of my early team meetings in Washington. He also agreed to meet with each team member, one on one, over the following five days. I had everyone scheduled until the last day, when I simply did not have anyone left. I felt so embarrassed and apologized to him profusely. Jimmy was so gracious and said, "Don't worry about it; let's go have coffee at Starbucks anyway."

We did, and it was incredible. I was fairly well known in our small community, and as we sat drinking our coffee, people would come in and say hi to me. I would introduce them to Jimmy, and he would take it from there. It was wonderful; he made everyone feel special, and I learned a great deal by watching him and seeing how quickly people warmed to him and his stories. By spending time with him, I've come to know that the most important thing to attract leaders is having a great attitude.

Don't spend time with negative people. A great attitude is contagious.

Books and CDs

Books are amazing. I have spent a lifetime reading books on psychology, motivation, and human performance. I am known for handing out books; in fact, I think I hand out more books than business cards. I give books to my team, prospects, friends, and clients. Even in the days before I joined network marketing, I would give books on psychology to my hair salon clients. At the back of this book is a list of some of the great books I have read over and over.

A great book to get you started is The Magic of Thinking Big, by Dr. David Schwartz.

He believes that the main thing holding people back is the relative smallness of their thoughts, and he explains the importance of "thinking positively toward oneself." He begins the book by relating a story of a salesman who sold significantly more product and made more money than his coworkers. Schwartz points out that the man was not smarter, more educated, or better connected than his colleagues; he just had a different set of expectations. He expected to sell more, so he did.

Today, just about every great book is also available on CD. I recommend that you buy the book and the CD so that you can read and underline important points and listen to the CD when you are on the treadmill or driving. Reinforcement is invaluable. While commuting to work, use the CDs as your traveling library. Eventually you will build your own library of personal development books and CDs.

There are several related topics worth researching and learning more about:

- Body language
- People skills
- Personality types
- Communication
- Leadership
- Relationship building
- Storytelling
- Time management

Once you start reading these books, you will start thinking these thoughts and believing these beliefs.

Web/Internet

The Internet provides free access to an unlimited number of personal development blogs and websites. There are also thousands of online courses and at-home study courses on personal development. Online masterminds and study groups are also available, but these usually have a fee associated with them.

Ask your networking colleagues or just spend a few hours searching the Internet, and you will be overwhelmed with the amount of terrific information freely available.

Stop and Smell the Roses

You are on a lifelong journey of personal growth, and every now and then you should take time out and enjoy the changes in your life. Sometimes these changes just creep up on you.

Joni and I used to travel everywhere on the cheap. One night, we were in this hotel room that was so smoky Joni had toilet paper stuffed up her nose. In the middle of the night, she woke up and said, "What is wrong with us?"

At this time, we were both making about seven to eight thousand dollars a month. Joni said, "We can get a hotel room anywhere—what are we doing?" It was one of those aha moments. We were so focused on growing our businesses and having fun that we hadn't realized that they really were growing and we were changing our lives.

From time to time, you've got to stop for a moment to smell the roses and remember back to where you were a year ago. Remember where you were before you started to dream. Try to remember all of those things so that you can appreciate how far you have come. In the early years I never smelled the roses, but I certainly do now.

Leadership Development

To become a leader worth following, you must give time and attention to the inner man. To leave a legacy that goes beyond accomplishment alone, a leader must devote himself to matters of the heart.

—Andy Stanley, *The Next Generation of Leaders*

You will grow into your leadership role, and the people who join your team will also grow into leadership roles. The most important aspect about being a leader in network marketing is that you are a leader of a volunteer army. The people on your team are independent business owners, not your employees, and as such, leading them is best done by example and encouragement.

Dealing with different personalities on your team is an ongoing challenge, but it is necessary. You are here to help them move toward their dreams, and in so doing you will move toward yours. I suggest reading some books on personality types and communication. I have listed some great books in the references section.

> *We set young leaders up for a fall if we encourage them to envision what they can do before they consider what kind of person they can be.*
>
> *—Ruth Barton*

Heartfelt Network Marketing leaders care about their team members' dreams and aspirations. It is exciting to learn what motivates your team members and inspire them to stay the course. Sometimes this is easier said than done.

I have over one hundred thousand members in my downline, and unfortunately there is no way I will ever be able to help each member personally. This bothered me for a long time because I live for the opportunity to help people grow and build their dreams. Ultimately, my passion to serve empowered me to write this book and introduce you to the Heartfelt Network Marketing principles. Through this book and the following nationwide series of Heartfelt Network Marketing seminars, I can at least convey to everyone who wants to grow the principles that allowed me to become a millionaire and one of the happiest people I know.

I once heard a speaker on stage explain how we know when we are a leader.

> *Look behind. If there is anyone behind you, then you are a leader. If nobody's following you, go back and head them up from the back and then move into the middle and allow somebody else to have that leadership in front of you.*
>
> *—Unknown*

I realized that you can lead from the middle, the back, or even the front, and inside of that you're a leader.

Heartfelt Network Marketing leaders are role models and mentors to their team, and most of all, the chief cheerleader.

If your team is growing and you always think you have to be the top banana and not let them shine, then you're not a Heartfelt Network Marketing leader. We acknowledge natural talent, and when we have a natural leader on our team, we celebrate him, open the way for him, and get out of his way. You need to be humble enough to cheer him on and let him shine. He may be bigger than you, and that is the beauty of this industry. You should never try holding a natural leader back. When Joni finally joined my current company, it only took her two years to pass me, and I had been working with the company for four years. I celebrated when she sped past me, and thanks to her great leadership qualities, we have eight consecutive millionaires in one leg. I cheered every one of them on from my heart.

A sign of a great leader is attracting people better than yourself.

A leader is constantly growing and nurturing team members. You have to work as a team to build a company and become a team of millionaires. Growth takes more than one person. No one person or situation will make it for you.

You need a team to fulfill your obligations.

Build your team with leaders—help by inspiring them, providing reading materials and links to personal development information, and being there when they have questions. Set the example, but remember you are unique and you can't be all things to all people. Don't expect them to do what you are not willing to do.

Being a leader is a commitment to your team, because you won't get to where you want to be without helping them get where they want to be. Network marketing is about constant growth, both personal and financial. Every now and then an exceptional person has come my way and I have paid for them to attend company events until they are on their feet. This is not always doable, so of course use your own judgment, but a generous spirit is very rewarding. Often I will travel to wherever I am needed to support team members. This is my business *and* theirs.

Stay engaged with your team members; celebrating with your team is important.

When possible, involve your team in meeting the top achievers. You will find that just meeting them will inspire and energize your team. It will also make them feel good about themselves because you are so proud of them that you want the top achievers to know your team.

A valuable lesson to learn is to know who deserves your time and support. When I get behind someone it is all the way, and I have learned that sometimes the only thing the person produces is hot air. I know it sounds harsh, but it's the truth. You'll have many team members who will genuinely put in the work; these are the people you should be concentrating on. These days, I test my intuition and the team member by setting a few small goals for the person. If she delivers, then we are on; if not, I explain that if you take a step, I will take a step; if you take two steps, I will take two steps.

Growth applies to you as a person and as a team leader. In network marketing, we are all leaders at different stages of growth, and it is up to us to lead by example and grow our team.

You have to grow them so they can become successful leaders.

—*Stan Barker*

Your Alternative to Growth

Be not afraid of growing slowly; be afraid only of standing still.

—*Chinese Proverb*

If you're not going up, you're going down. There is no standing still. The alternative to growth is stagnation and depression. So many men and women in America are depressed from doing nothing and believing they have no control over the lives. Consequently, they sit in front of a screen and become zombies, feeding on reality TV. Even I would end up depressed if I did that all day long, day in day out.

Heartfelt Network Marketing gives you all the tools you need to get back in the race and do it at your pace, but you are in with a chance.

This time next year, do you want to be in the same situation you are in now? If you keep going without making a change to yourself or some aspect of your life, you will be even worse off than you are now, because the rest of us will have moved on and left you behind.

I can't guarantee where you'll be in a year's time, but I can guarantee that a year will have passed. It is up to you to determine where you will be and what your life will be like.

Do you love yourself and your family enough to stand up and get going? I hope so.

Every pro was once an amateur, every expert was once a beginner, and every network marketing top achiever was once where you are. Dream big and start now. The sooner you start, the sooner you will create great changes in your life.

- Don't be afraid of not knowing — be afraid of not learning.
- Don't be afraid of getting it wrong — be afraid of not trying.
- Don't be afraid of coming last — be afraid of not being in the race.

Most people don't give themselves enough time. You've got to work hard, not for a few weeks or a few months, but for a few years. It takes three to five years to establish yourself in business. The first two years of any business are nothing but survival time. (Remember the unwritten law that the first eighteen months in business, everything turns into a mess.)

—Art Williams, **All You Can Do Is All You Can Do**

Belief in Yourself, Your Product, and Your Company

Heartfelt Belief

> *The power of belief, the absolutely awesome incredible power of belief, is the genie in your life. Let me say that again: the absolutely awesome and incredible power of your belief is the genie in your life.*
>
> —*Eldon Taylor,* **I Believe**

Belief is defined as a state or habit of mind in which trust or confidence is placed in some person or thing.

A belief is something that you believe to be true. It is personal, and what you believe could very well be quite different from what the next person believes. Beliefs come in all shapes and sizes; some will last a lifetime, and others will be abandoned or updated as you learn more about life.

A belief is not a thought or a feeling—it is a deep-rooted knowing on your behalf. We start creating our beliefs from the time we are born. Our initial beliefs are formed by input from our parents and other authority figures like teachers and grandparents. We may have observed an event or been told something repetitively, and over time our thoughts and opinions regarding this becomes a belief which takes root in our subconscious. Quite often some of our core beliefs are a direct result of what our parents told us to believe when we were children.

Beliefs can be empowering or crippling.

A close friend of mine spent the first half of her adult life believing that her place in life was to be the second in command, or the person behind the scenes. She believed that she was a second-class person, and that meant she was not born to be the CEO or the star performer. This toxic belief was instilled into her by her loving mother. Every morning, her mother would kneel down, kiss her little daughter lovingly on the cheek, and remind her that she was a second-class person because she was half Chinese and half Australian. She thought she was protecting her little girl by reminding her to be mindful of her position and to always be quiet and well behaved. She hoped that by keeping a low profile, her little girl would get through the day without being teased and ridiculed. As you can see, sometimes a negative belief can be passed on with a loving intention.

Fortunately for some of us, including my friend, as we grow older we start to formulate our own beliefs based on our experience of the world. We may even start to question some of our core beliefs.

One of the characteristics of beliefs is that they are self-fulfilling—once we have the thought planted into our subconscious, we naturally set about collecting information and observations to validate and substantiate it.

Whether you think you can, or you think you can't—you're right.

—Henry Ford

Belief is a very powerful force and is a double-edged sword. Beliefs have the power to catapult you into an exciting, adventurous life or confine you to a hole in the wall.

Beliefs are far more powerful than thoughts and transient states of mind. A belief can take you to the end of the earth—it did for Columbus. Against the entire population of the world at the time, he believed the world was round, and he risked the life of his crew and himself to follow his belief.

I believed that network marketing was my ticket to freedom in every sense of the word. My belief in the system and in the unlimited financial rewards available to me was so strong that I ignored the pressure from my well-meaning but uninformed family and friends to stop. Every time my tenure with a network company ended, I just picked myself up and continued on, looking for "a home." I never doubted the networking industry or the system of network marketing. I never doubted the financials, because they were based on mathematics that left no room for doubt or interpretation. I never doubted that given enough time I would succeed, because I simply *would not quit*. My beliefs are what fueled my perseverance and kept me moving forward to financial freedom and a wonderful life filled with choices for my children and grandchildren.

It is my continual belief in network marketing as an honorable profession that keeps me going today. I want the world to know that there is a way to build a great business on your own terms and help others at the same time.

There are many stories about the incredible power of belief, and one of the most famous is about the four-minute mile. People around the world believed that it was impossible to run a mile in less than four minutes until 1954 when Roger Bannister ran it in three minutes and 59.4 seconds. Incredible as it may seem, as soon as Roger disproved the belief, hundreds of people changed their belief and also ran a sub-four-minute mile. These people did not suddenly turn into a different species or discover a super food; they simply learned that their belief about the four-minute mile was no longer valid and created a new belief that they could run a mile in less than four minutes. I don't mean that they instantly developed into world-class runners; I mean they believed they could do it, so they set about training and working toward their goal to break that barrier.

We often experience a similar belief barrier in network marketing. It's called the millionaire ceiling. People don't believe it can be done until someone on their team does it.

In my downline, we have eight millionaires in a row. Each one personally enrolled the next one. The first person breaks the million-dollar barrier, and then all of a sudden two or three more break through, and it just keeps happening.

Seeing your colleagues break through is inspiring and adds fuel to your fire. From my personal experience, it feels great to know that I had a part in helping many people become six-figure earners and millionaires. That success will affect generations to come.

I often wonder what would have happened if I had said no.

Beliefs can also be limiting, in that they stop us from doing things that we dream about or give us a crippling filter through which we experience the world. Many common limiting beliefs are so prevalent that we don't even question them. They are as invisible as oxygen and nearly as powerful.

They inflict extreme control over our life without us being aware of it. How many of these common negative beliefs have you come across?

- Money doesn't grow on trees.
- Dreams are a waste of time.
- Don't get ahead of yourself.
- I have no chance of ever getting ahead.
- It's too late to change.
- I'm too old to start again.
- I will never amount to anything.
- The rich get richer, and the poor get poorer.
- Network marketing is a get rich quick scheme.
- High-pressure selling is a requirement of network marketing.
- Getting out of here is never going to happen—I come from the wrong side of the tracks.

Most of these negative beliefs may not stop you from dreaming, but they probably will stop you from living your dream. If you believe that the rich get richer and the poor get poorer—and that you are in the poor category—you have an automatic excuse for not trying to change your situation. You believe it is a law of nature, so you don't try. You don't even question the validity of the belief.

Negative beliefs don't have to be true; in fact most of the time they are passing comments which over time we take it on face value as being true.

If you believe that you are trying your hardest and no matter what you do, you never seem to be able to break through, you can envelop negative beliefs. Eventually, you believe that whatever you are trying to do will never happen and simply stop trying.

Often you don't look any further than yourself as the cause of failure, whereas it could be your environment or factors outside of your control. I parted from my first network marketing company with the belief that I had somehow let my friends and myself down. I lived with this belief for quite some time until I eventually realized that it was the company that let me down and that the outcome was outside of my control.

The flea training analogy is a great demonstration of how our beliefs are sometimes developed by events and circumstances that have nothing to do with us as individuals:

They say that a flea can naturally jump two hundred times its own height. But when you put fleas in a jar with a lid on, they jump and jump, constantly hitting the lid, until they eventually jump just short of the lid. The incredible thing is that when you take the lid off, they will not jump out of the jar. They have been trained to jump just shy of the lid, and that is all they can do. Their physical capabilities haven't changed, but their belief has.

If you believe you can or you believe you can't, either way you will be correct. This is why it is so very important to work on believing in yourself.

Your beliefs about yourself and your position in the world around you govern your experience of the world. If you believe that you are invisible and unimportant in the overall scheme of things, eventually your physical appearance and the way you walk, sit, and talk will reflect this. Your personal presence will shrink to match your belief about yourself, and people's opinion of you will follow suit, and the downward spiral goes on.

The wonderful aspect about beliefs is that you have the power to change them. Once you become aware of your limiting beliefs and the impact they have on your dreams, you can start to replace them with empowering beliefs.

As you begin to understand the fixed and growth mindsets, you will see exactly how one thing leads to another—how a belief that your qualities are carved in stone leads to a host of thoughts and actions, and how a belief that your qualities can be cultivated leads to a host of different thoughts and actions, taking you down an entirely different road.

—Carol Dweck, **Fixed and Growth Mindsets**

Believing in Yourself

You may succeed if nobody else believes in you, but you will never succeed if you don't believe in yourself. Owning a dream means having your belief in yourself outweigh your fears.

—John Maxwell

This is the start of everything. You have to believe in yourself if you are ever going to take control of your future. Now that you understand a little about beliefs and the power they have over your life, it is time to look at what your personal beliefs are and to work out if you need to do some rethinking.

Awareness is the first step in harnessing the power of belief.

This is a very important step in moving toward your dream. Starting at the top, here are the questions to ask yourself:

- Do you believe you are worthy of your dream?
- Do you believe you deserve your dream?
- Do you feel confident that you have what it takes to overcome fear, doubt, criticism, and the thousand and one other road blocks that instantly occur when you set out to achieve your dream?
- What do you say to yourself about yourself?
- How do you refer to yourself when talking to others?
- What pet phrases do you have that describe yourself or your world?
- What do you habitually say about money, other people, and your future?
- What do you believe about network marketing?
- What do you believe about your career as a network marketer?

The quickest way to work out what you believe about yourself is to answer each of these questions and write down your answers. Don't rush it; give it some serious thought. You are working on your future. Your beliefs are the way to make your dreams reality.

If you are in a loving relationship, you might also ask your partner to answer these questions, as they relate to you. Quite often, we are not aware of our pet phrases or attitudes because they come from our subconscious, but our friends and family are fully aware and are usually very willing to enlighten us. A separate, more illuminating exercise would be for both of you to work through this exercise. It would be interesting to know your partner's beliefs as well. Building a dream can be a team event, but sometimes we allow our loved ones' beliefs to overrule our own.

Self-belief is the most powerful factor in achieving your dream, regardless of the size of your dream. If you believe you are addicted to chocolate, then it is likely you will not be able to go to bed at night leaving the last piece of chocolate in the cupboard. If your parents raised you to believe that you can do anything, you will plow through every barrier knowing without a doubt that you will realize your dream of becoming a millionaire.

I believed in my ability to work hard and care for my family, and when I finally reached the magic six-figure income, I believed I was unstoppable.

I felt strong and knew I was going to the top. I could see it. I could see myself in the Winner's Circle. All I had to do was work hard and maintain belief in myself and the network marketing system. I saw hundreds of everyday people with many challenges making it big; this continually reinforced my belief.

Chances are you have a mix of empowering and limiting beliefs. Taking into consideration your plan to achieve your dreams, answer the following questions:

- What limiting beliefs would be beneficial to drop?
- What new empowering beliefs would be beneficial to develop?

- What empowering beliefs do you currently have?

Beliefs are affected by your environment and the people you regularly associate with. Ask yourself the following:

- Is your home environment helping or hindering your empowering beliefs and your ability to change them?
- Is your work environment helping or hindering your empowering beliefs and your ability to change them?
- Are your family and friends supportive or saboteurs of your empowering beliefs and your ability to change them?

These are not easy questions to ask or answer. However, to give yourself every chance of success you may want to at least be aware of any aspect of your life that is stopping you from moving forward. Even if you can't or don't want to do anything about some of your less than helpful beliefs, colleagues, or situations, at least you will be aware of them and you can take steps to dilute the negative influence they have over you.

Tips on Raising Your Self-Belief

Believing in yourself is a choice and an attitude.

If you are primarily a pessimist, you will want to work on moving the needle toward becoming an optimist. This is not easy, but it is your choice to either see your future abundant with wonderful possibilities or overwhelmed by misery and disappointment. No one is forcing you to take the negative route. True, you may venture forward on the road toward your dream and encounter disappointment along the way, but once you are on your journey and you keep your dream in focus, the chances are you will find ways to keep going. Choosing to take responsibility for your life and accepting that there is something you can do about it is both exhilarating and terrifying — exhilarating because you can leave your baggage at the door and step into a future designed and built by you, and terrifying because you have to step up and walk the talk. You have to face your fears and work through them. You have to accept that you may not succeed quickly and that there will be lessons to learn, but what is the alternative?

Getting started is the hard part. I didn't find starting on my path to freedom an issue because I was hungry and I am naturally a glass half full person, but there were times when things were not working out the way I had planned that caused me to stop for a minute and consider my situation. I decided that I was committed to my journey, and I believed I was on the right path. I took a good, hard look at the alternative of a lifetime of money worries and restrictions on what I could and couldn't afford and compared this to my dream of freedom. I believed that all I had to do was stay focused and work through every obstacle and I would get there…and I did.

I am not some special, gifted superwoman. I was a teenage mother, a hair stylist, a wife, and a high school dropout, but I was not a quitter.

I had a dream to pursue, and most of all I had to prove to myself that I could succeed.

Thinking about the alternative to your dream is a great way to get you moving, because we humans will do more to avoid pain than we will ever do for pleasure. So if your dream doesn't motivate you to change your attitude, think about the ugly alternative.

One of the greatest limiting beliefs is self-doubt. I experienced self-doubt when it came to my ability as a parent. I was just a teenager when I had my daughter and twenty-one when Justin came along. I dreamed of being the best parent in the world. My expectations were so high, in fact, that I didn't think I was even a good parent. This belief caused me to seek advice from books and parenting classes, which were great, but I also relied heavily on a friend for advice. I followed her instructions to the letter, which went against my nature, but my self-doubt was so great that I did as I was told. This is a sad but important lesson; self-doubt causes us to stop thinking for ourselves and let others make our decisions for us.

From personal experience I highly recommend Landmark Education as a way to work through your limiting beliefs and put the past where it belongs: behind you!

If you are having trouble believing in yourself, maybe you could do some reflecting:

> Have you ever been successful at something in the past? If so, what was it and how did it feel? Can you remember what it took to become successful at it? Sometimes success in one area allows you to transfer that belief to a new area.
>
> What are you passionate about? How do you feel when you are involved with this passion? Do you get excited and experience a feeling of strength?
>
> Think of all the things in the past that you have done exceptionally well—anything that made you feel good about yourself or that someone thanked or complimented you for.
>
> The important thing is to work on creating a list of achievements that you can focus on rather than the feeling of failure. The achievements can be anything and any size; you

will be surprised how a bunch of little achievements add up to something significant.

Your success depends mainly upon what you think of yourself and whether you believe in yourself.

—*William J. H. Boetcker*

Belief in Your Product and the Company

I covered this in the chapter titled The Fundamentals of the Network Marketing Industry. You must believe in the company you are building your business with. It is vital that the company's values and ethics are in alignment with your own. You are betting on this company and their products and services to help you reach your dreams, so do your research thoroughly.

Section III

Building Your Business

If I had to do it all over again, rather than build an old-style type business, I would have started building a network marketing business.

—*Robert Kiyosaki*

The Core Steps to Building Your Business

What do you want to be doing this time next year, or in five or ten years from now?

No matter what you do, the one thing that you have no control over is time.

I recently participated in a team call for a friend, Jay Bennett, and he compared life to a football game. He said, "Reality is you will be in the final quarter and then the last ten seconds."

Which quarter are you in now?

The sooner you start working toward your dreams the sooner your future will change. One of the greatest benefits of building a network marketing business and developing your residual income stream is the easy start-up process. Unlike traditional businesses, you can start building within days or even hours from the instant you decide on which network marketing company resonates with you.

There are thirteen basic steps:

1. Research and select the type of product or service you want to share. Personally, I like a product that is visual or emotional that I can try for myself. Your own story of using the product or service to successfully overcome a challenge is always a great starter. Think about how you look for personal reviews on the Internet and from your friends with

regards to movies, restaurants, diets, and so forth. Products that give you the chance to have a before and after photo are always good.

2. Next, find a networking company that distributes the type of product or service you want to work with. Remember to check out the company's structure, compensation plan, culture, and track record with associates.

3. Study the company growth path and write up a business plan that highlights milestones and upcoming events.

   Steps 1, 2, and 3 are covered in more detail in the chapter titled The Fundamentals of the Network Marketing Industry.

4. Work on your *why*. What is the challenge you had to overcome or the dream that drives you?

   You will find more information on discovering your why in the chapter titled Heartfelt Dreaming, Hope, and the Ugly Alternative.

5. Practice telling your *story*. You are not limited to just telling your story. You can also tell other people's stories. In the beginning, that's all I had, but even today sometimes I will tell someone else's story because I know it will resonate with my prospect.

6. Develop meaningful *relationships* with like-minded people, other network professionals, and centers of influence. Heartfelt Network Marketing is founded on great relationships.

7. Start building your list. Look at who the people are in your contact list on your phone and your computer. Check out your Facebook friends and fans.

8. *Attract* prospects and new friends by developing your professional profile as an *authority* in your field. It is more enjoyable to share your

story with people who come to you wanting to know more.

9. Take advantage of *technology* to spread your story, raise your profile as an authority in your chosen field, connect with like-minded people globally, and show others that you are working toward your dream.

10. Remember to have *fun*. This business is your choice, so make it enjoyable and fun. You get to pick your team members and work out the plays, so have fun with it while you are growing.

11. *Recruit* like-minded people to build with you. You are building a legacy for your family, so make sure you recruit people who will help you build and whom you can help in return. Keep your inner circle filled with like-minded people you love to be around and would love to travel with.

12. Don't get discouraged if people don't show up immediately or if they decline your offer. People lead you to other people, so soon you will have a network of people who will lead you to someone you would never meet any other way. It only takes a couple of inspired and excited people in your business to get it moving.

13. Follow through with your team and support their growth.

You don't build a business—you build people—and then people build the business.

—Zig Ziglar

Recruiting

Recruiting great people to join your business is pivotal to your success.

The law of reciprocity works very well for recruiting. If you show a genuine interest in others, they will want to know more about you.

It is up to you to start the relationship-building process, and this is best done by asking questions and then zipping up and listening to the person's answer.

Taking a few minutes to find commonalities in interests, family, hobbies, work, children, friends, beliefs, and more is a powerful way to connect with people and begin the connection process.

A simple way to remember this process is: FORM

> **F** = Family and friend—people love to talk about themselves.
>
> **O** = Occupation—find out what they do for a living.
>
> **R** = Recreation and hobbies—ask what they do for fun.
>
> **M** = Mission or message—discover what they believe in and are passionate about; what their main interests are.

If there is something you would like someone to know, but you don't want to make a statement, you can ask the person a leading question so that his or her response will give you the opportunity to say what is on your mind.

Do everything in your power to make the other person feel comfortable—in other words, make sure to address any anxiety or concerns they may have.

Heartfelt Network Marketing is centered on building relationships and helping people through storytelling. The most successful business builders are usually great storytellers.

Starting out by building a relationship with your prospect allows you to understand their why and evaluate their storytelling skills. A great way to find storytellers is to ask your prospect if he or she knows a good storyteller. Just by asking the question, you will open up the communication channel, because invariably your prospect will be curious as to the relevance of storytelling and ask you to explain.

Here are other great questions to ask your prospect:

- Who do you know who has been in networking?
- Do you know any network marketers?

Recruiting and educating are ongoing key tasks in building your people and your business.

Never stop recruiting.

Heartfelt Network Marketing Is a Storytelling Business

Talk to someone about themselves and they'll listen for hours.

—Dale Carnegie, **How to Win Friends & Influence People**

We all love listening to stories, and nearly everyone can tell a story, especially about their own lives and experiences. How often have you struck up a conversation with a complete stranger sitting next to you on a flight to somewhere and ended up telling her your life story or listened to hers? We love talking about ourselves—anytime and anywhere. This should tell you something: if you start the conversation with a noninvasive question or a little story and then wait a second or two, the other person will quickly take over the conversation, and all you have to do is focus and actively listen.

When meeting someone new, take it slowly and give the other person the stage. The most important thing you can do is to focus on him and listen. Don't allow your eyes to wonder or interrupt him. Don't hold your breath waiting for your chance to say something. I am sure you don't like it when someone asks you a question and then scans the room looking for a bigger catch, or looks like he is about to burst if he doesn't say something soon.

Your body language can tell stories you would probably prefer to keep to yourself, so practice and genuinely be engaged in the conversation.

Most people love to talk about their lives and experiences because the memories and thoughts just come flooding in. They don't have to think about it so they will feel more relaxed and comfortable with you.

If you can ask a question and then step back and listen intently to the answer, you are well on your way.

The more the other person talks, the more you will learn about what is important to her and where her concerns are. You can't help someone if you don't know what it is she needs help with.

Storytelling is a key Heartfelt Network Marketing skill. Storytelling is the most comfortable nonthreatening way to connect to another person, and most people can tell a story.

Your story shouldn't be as long as *War and Peace*. It is a fast world today, and unfortunately people get bored quickly, so be aware of how long you are taking and of their body language. I have become pretty good at noticing when the other person's eyes start to glaze over or when he is obviously looking for an escape route. As soon as you notice these little body language messages, cut it short and hand the stage back to him.

Telling your story helps to break down barriers, but make sure that you tell a story relevant to the topic you are discussing.

Eventually the time may come when the other person starts to ask direct business opportunity questions. It could take three or four interactions, or three or four years, but when it does, lead with your story, not a string of facts and figures. Depending on the relevancy, I might tell people about being a teenage mom and working toward financial freedom that was never going to eventuate until I found network marketing, or how I was very overweight and thanks to a particular product I dropped three dress sizes in thirty days, or how this wonderful profession has helped grow my family in so many ways. The story I tell depends on who I am speaking to.

> *One story is worth ten thousand facts. Don't just throw out facts, tell a story. Your prospects and distributors will remember the story long after the facts have been forgotten. And stories are more powerful and more motivating. Don't you want to inspire your prospect or distributor? I bet you can remember an interesting story told to you by your first-grade teacher. But you have probably forgotten 90 percent of the facts you had to memorize in high school. Proof enough? And the best part is that stories engage people. When you are telling a story, people forget about you. They focus on the story. So if you want people to stop judging you and to focus on the opportunity, tell a story.*
>
> —Big Al, **Big Al's Sponsoring Magic**

Rather than spending time in the beginning studying and practicing "the close," I suggest you work on your story. Get it down to a couple of minutes that get your message across in a heartfelt way. It's also good to have a twenty- to thirty-second statement that creates curiosity about what it is that you do.

Sometimes we get overexcited about our products, services, or opportunity and barrage people with facts and figures that they just don't want to know about. This is often referred to as verbal vomit, and it generally results in the other person wanting to get away from you as quickly as possible.

It is a good idea to let people peek into your lifestyle without bragging. Simply being quietly confident and caring more about what the other person wants to talk about sometimes allows the other person to open up more and hear your message. She will feel that you really care about what she wants, and at her own pace, she can start to believe that you can help her.

✳ The power of your story gives people hope and the chance to dream again. Sharing your story is more important than leading with facts and figures.

Facts tell. Stories sell.

—*Big Al,* **How to Prospect, Sell and Build Your Network Marketing Business with Stories**

Telling a personal story is when you become expressive, candid, and heartfelt. Your story doesn't have to be a rock concert. It can be a few words, but you will be surprised how it can give the other person hope and lift him up long enough to start thinking.

All it took for me to change my entire future was hearing other average people tell their stories of how they went from hopelessness to having a future of their making. I realized that if they were doing it, then so could I.

Everyone needs role models and needs to meet people who have succeeded. I realized that my job was to infuse hope into others who had given up, and I did this through telling my story.

Sometimes all it takes is to show the other person that they have options. When someone travels through life with her head down, it is nearly impossible to see what is up ahead unless someone like you helps her look up. Chances are she is overwhelmed with the stress of her day job, which she doesn't even like anymore; she feels helpless because she has kids and responsibilities and even if she could get out she doesn't know where to go.

Listening to your stories will give her hope even if you have only just started your journey. It doesn't matter where you are in your life's story, the point is you are doing something about it, which means she can too. Sometime it works even better if you are just starting out, because the person can more easily relate to you and you are more sensitive to how she is feeling.

Your library of stories will grow as you do.

I was so excited when I bought my first house, because I knew that when people heard about it, they were going to say, "I can do that too."

Then I bought my mom a condo, which was huge for me. She lived in a tiny apartment, but she had to shovel walks and go down icy steps to her car, which she had to park in the open. I asked her if she would be open to moving if I found her a place with a garage and charged her less rent than she was paying currently, and she agreed. I couldn't afford to buy the condo outright yet, so we agreed that she would pay $600 a month, which was $150 less than her current rent. But as my business grew, it wasn't long before I took over the payments and she no longer had to pay rent. She now has this fabulous condo with a double car garage and garage opener, which was the biggest thing. It makes me happy knowing she is safe in her own home without any payments. She is eighty-four years old now and still very productive.

I love it. It was just inches. My story wasn't an overnight rags-to-riches story. I was growing myself and my business inch by inch. It took me more than ten years to reach millionaire status, but if I had kept styling hair, no matter how hard I worked, I would never have become a millionaire.

I no longer consider what I do hard work—rather it is **heart** *work.*

It is wonderful seeing my kids grow into great young adults and being able to help them reap the rewards of the life-changing decision I made over a decade ago.

You can also use other people's stories to relate and demonstrate a point. In fact, using a variety of people's stories may help validate your position with your prospect. I use another person's story when I feel that it will resonate with my prospect more than my personal story. However, until people are ready to listen and consider change it doesn't matter how great your story is because the time is just not right for them. You must come to grips with this and not be emotionally attached to the outcome.

You can't say the right thing to the wrong person and you can't say the wrong thing to the right person.

—*Anonymous*

Remind yourself that it is not about you or your great offer, it is about the other person. Consider leaving them with this great quote:

Imagine a new story for your life and start living it.

—*Paulo Coelho*

Creating Mutually Rewarding Relationships

It's not enough to have a dream. You must also have a dream team. People recognize this truth in sports. They understand that they cannot win without the right players. But it also applies to every other aspect of life. If you want to achieve your dream, you need others willing to come alongside you and work with you.

—John Maxwell

Relationships are a very important aspect of life. The most important relationship is the one you have with yourself. As I said earlier in the book, people take their cues from you. If you stand straight and feel good about yourself and your story, people will respond to you accordingly and open the communication channel. It is a must to believe in what you are doing and who you are.

Relationships start when you develop rapport with another, and they come in all shapes and sizes. Some people will stay for a while and others will pass on through. The length of time you spend with others is not as important as the quality of the relationship you develop.

Rapport: a close and harmonious relationship in which the people or groups concerned understand each other's feelings or ideas and communicate well.

—**The New Oxford American Dictionary**

In your network marketing world, you have a wide variety of relationships above and beyond your personal relationships with your family and friends.

- Upline/Sponsor
- Company Owners and Executives
- Top Achievers
- Peers
- Team Members
- Prospects
- Customers
- Social Media
- Advocates, Supporters, and Fans
- Groups
- Audience

Regardless of the type of relationship, it is imperative that you always be a person of integrity and sincerity. Heartfelt Network Marketers are by definition genuine, caring, and honest people.

If you go looking for a friend, you're going to find they're scarce. If you go out to be a friend, you'll find them everywhere.

—Zig Ziglar

You are building a business, so it is a good idea to pick your relationships wisely; you pretty much have to fall in love with them.

Speaking of falling in love, I met my wonderful husband, Dr. Scott Peterson, through network marketing. Scott is an Internet marketing wizard and a couple of years ago he approached me with regards to raising my profile on the Internet. Long story short, we married in 2013, and now I am his number one client.

Traditionally, most network marketing promotion and recruitment has been via personal meetings and a great deal of one on one personal contact. This is certainly how I started out, but thanks to Scott I have added social media and attraction marketing to my business-building strategy. I will talk more about technology later in this section.

Forming relationships is the part I like most because it is no fun going to a party by yourself.

Making new friends every step of the way is fun.

It is imperative to overcome any shyness or reluctance you may have in dealing with people, because you won't be able to help them if you can't relate to them and them to you.

I started working as a hair stylist at a very young age, and I was painfully shy. My first mentor explained to me that if I wanted to earn money and do people's hair, I had to overcome my shyness and make people comfortable and confident in my chair. It was difficult at the start, but I was motivated by the fact that I only got paid if I had happy return clients.

I quickly became comfortable talking to the ladies who came into the salon, but with the advent of the hippie era, we had young men coming into the salon because they were worried that their barber would cut their hair too short. I was still a young girl at the time, and I had no idea what to say to these young men. In desperation, I asked another fellow stylist and she said just ask them about their favorite sports team and you won't have to say another word—and she was right.

It takes time to develop a relationship. My experience has shown that it takes about three interactions before both sides start to feel truly comfortable with each other. Sometimes you will hit it off with someone immediately, and on other occasions you may never click. You just never know until you give it a go.

Ask your prospect to tell you his story so that you can see if there is anything he needs help with and if you are capable of providing that help. Remember, when interacting with your prospect it is all about him.

Early on, I destroyed many relationships as a result of going into network marketing conversations without learning anything about the other person. I must have come across like a snake oil salesman on speed. I burned many of my friends and probably a few hairstyling clients.

I have found that the best way to create relationships with people is to be someone you would like to meet. Be interesting, polite, upbeat, and relaxed; radiate positive energy; and most of all, be a great listener.

Be the kind of person you enjoy meeting and relating to.

To help you on your way, try these suggestions:

- Learn about the group or person you are going to meet prior to your meeting. Google and Facebook are great ways to do background research. People buy from those they like and trust, and trust is built through shared values and genuine understanding. Prior to attending a network or association meeting, do some homework and learn about the industry.

Knowledge is king.

- In the beginning, I got a lot more nos than yeses, but there were enough yeses that it surprised me. It always surprised me. I think Joni and I attracted people to us because we were so excited. You have to get excited, and we did.

People are attracted to energy and fun.

- Create a list of three or four questions you could ask when the time is right that give the other person an opportunity to talk about themselves.

- Always practice active listening. Focus on the other person while they are speaking to you. Don't let your eyes stray around the room; keep them on the person in front of you. Just think how annoyed you get when someone you are talking to is searching the room for their next catch rather than genuinely listening to you.

Most people do not listen with the intent to understand; they listen with the intent to reply.

—Stephen R. Covey

- Don't overwhelm the other person by telling her everything at your first encounter. Let her speak more than you, and when it is your turn, give her little tidbits that will motivate her to ask for more or seek you out at the next event because she wants to know more. Remember, you need to know what her dreams and issues are before you can begin to help.

- In your relationships, you need to be aware of timing and be sensitive enough to back up when you recognize that it may not be the right time. Eventually the person might come through the other side, and because of your sensitivity he may in fact call you and ask you about the thing you were trying to tell him a while ago.

Sometimes it might be the right solution but simply the wrong time.

Conflict

A mutually rewarding business-building relationship is personal, professional, value creating, and built on trust. Unfortunately it is not always smooth sailing, and there will be times when you are going to have to deal with conflict of some type. I have never been good when it comes to conflict of any nature, and I have to admit that ignoring the problem and hoping that it will sort itself out or disappear was not the smartest thing to do.

Over the years, I have learned that the best way to handle issues or misunderstandings is upfront and immediate.

Speedy conflict resolution is very important in a team environment. There is a saying that bad news spreads many times faster than good news, and so does discontent. You want to keep your team concentrating on moving forward and not let it get sidetracked by someone's issues.

You will find that in most cases, clearing the air before it grows out of all proportion will turn the whole problem around, and it may even reinforce your relationship.

Understanding People

I found the *Birth Order Book* by Dr. Kevin Leman a great help when it came to understanding people. I often play a little game with myself and try to guess when the person I am talking to was born relative to their brothers and sisters. Generally speaking, the book explains that the first born is usually a high achiever, the middle child relates to people, and the baby is into more fun and feels freer.

Read books on personality types and body language to help you better understand people. There are different approaches to engaging with each personality type. Learn to read people and be sensitive to what they are saying and, more importantly, how they are saying it.

Share your story with genuine emotion and be authentic. Try not to sound like a robot. You may be bored with your story because you have told it a thousand times, but the person listening to you has probably never heard it before. Remember, energy is very charismatic.

Relating to people requires feelings, patience, and active listening. Try to see the situation from the other person's position and ask questions about his or her regular job. One of the best ways to get the conversation moving along is to say something encouraging and complimentary about someone's day job. Everyone loves to talk about work, whether it's good or bad. They may even tell you how bored and disgruntled they are with their regular job, which opens the way for you to ask questions and suggest a possible alternative.

If your prospect is showing symptoms of low self-esteem, try to bring them out gently by telling them about issues that you or someone you know had to overcome. Help them feel comfortable rather than overwhelmed or threatened.

The Three Foot Rule

I strongly disagree with the Three Foot Rule.

Anyone within three feet of you is someone you can talk to about your business opportunity or products.

What I do believe in, is that if it is appropriate, you should introduce yourself and strike up a conversation, giving the other person plenty of opportunity to talk about him or herself. Show genuine interest and ask noninvasive questions. Don't talk about your network marketing business until you are better acquainted and you believe that it will help the other person in some way.

You can make more friends in two months by becoming interested in other people than you can in two years by trying to get other people interested in you.

—*Dale Carnegie*

Not All Relationships Are Equal

Sometimes people use leverage for their own benefit. At my first company, Joni and I were bird dogs for an upline. He was the first big money earner we met. We found the prospects and handed them over to our upline, and he would sell them. He was a slick operator, and I learned a great deal about what not to do from him.

The Network Marketing Company

The friends and network marketing relationships I formed at each company were invaluable. The experiences—both good ones and the ones you would prefer to forget—will give you great memories.

Relationships take time to build; when you join a company, take your time and check it out thoroughly. Talk to other consultants as well as the top achievers, owners, and corporate executives before you start talking to your personal network.

I learned this lesson the hard way with my second company. It was a start-up with no track record, so there was really no investigating I could do. The company expanded quickly, and on the surface it looked good. I rushed in, and the product was great. I simply rode the wave for six months until several government agencies coordinated a seizure of all assets and bank accounts—all in one day. The whole experience ended badly for the company, my team, and myself, as well as the customers. Even though the company ended abruptly and sadly for all concerned, I made and kept some great, long-lasting relationships.

Stan Barker was one of the top achievers; he suggested that we should still meet weekly and continue to network and learn while we looked around for a new home. We were close, and we were a *team*. This level of support and depth of connectivity in our group ensured that we kept on growing and recovered quickly. In this profession, you are only alone if you choose to be.

Building Your Team

I'd rather have 1 percent of the effort of one hundred men than 100 percent of my own effort.

—J. Paul Getty

Building your business, or team, involves attracting like-minded people to join you. It is nearly impossible to build a dream on your own, but a group of people who are all inspired to grow their dreams can achieve powerful outcomes.

Help people see their dreams and give them hope through your personal stories. Remember, you are a great example of someone who has made the decision to take control of your life, and this will help the other person to start believing he or she can do it too. This is exactly how it happened for me.

Show your prospects how to change themselves and their future. Use the principals and processes outlined in Section II: Dreams, Hope, and the Ugly Alternative.

Focus on sharing information and working out how you and your offer can help your prospect in whatever area he or she has expressed as a dream, goal, or pain point. If the other person wants to know about the network marketing profession or your network marketing business, respond by asking what he or she would like to know first. Take it slowly, and don't jump straight into the traditional pitch mode. Drip-feeding the information makes it a two-way conversation rather than a one-way presentation. You will progressively uncover what is important to the other person.

Develop a list of the most common objections and your most successful responses. Ask others in your company how they have handled these types of objections and try their suggestions.

Sometimes the connection is just not there.

If you are not connecting with the other person, don't turn your connection into a last-ditch sales pitch. You won't relate to everyone you meet, and that is just how it goes, but there maybe someone on your team who will connect with the person; don't burn the connection.

Sometimes people just want to have fun and mix with positive, uplifting people. They want to follow the energy, and that is OK. They will meet other folks, and you never know who you will meet through them. You need to meet a lot of people, and every now and then a real go-getter will arrive and your team will take off again.

I learn new things every day. Here are a few of the important lessons I learned in recruiting and working with new people:

- When bringing on new people, make sure they are committed and worth your time and energy—give them some homework, just something small to see if they deliver. A lot of people are excited at the start, and then they realize that they have to do some work themselves. This tends to dampen their enthusiasm. This is fine, but don't fall into the trap that I did many times and that is doing the work for them with the hope that they will eventually takeover.

- Timing is everything in network marketing. You may have the answer to someone's prayers, but if it is not the right time for him or her, you just have to leave it and accept that it might not be the right time. Remember, Heartfelt Network Marketing is all about the other person.

Leadership

UNWRITTEN LAW: Most people can stay excited for two or three months. A few people can stay excited for two or three years. But a winner will stay excited for twenty or thirty years—or as long as it takes to win. If you're a leader of other people, you've got to set an example of being excited.

UNWRITTEN LAW: People won't follow a dull, disillusioned, frustrated crybaby.

—Art Williams, **All You Can Do Is All You Can Do**

Everyone has their own gifts; some people are extremely empowering and seem to be bigger than life; their charisma paves the way for their growth. People with this kind of charisma could lead an army, and there are others who lead by example and by teaching.

You can lead from the middle, the front, or the back, and inside of that you're a leader; sometimes you just have to lead from the front.

To grow your business, find leaders and support and promote them throughout your organization. You can't lead an army on your own, especially a volunteer army.

Advocates, Supporters, and Fans

Not everyone you meet or develop a relationship with will want to build a business. Some will be happy using the products and services, and others will become your greatest supporters and fans.

Long before I developed the principals of Heartfelt Network Marketing, I tried to convince my friend Jolee to join the industry. She kept saying no. I was so convinced that she would be brilliant that I kept trying.

She kept saying no. This went on for years until I finally gave in, but all during that time she helped me build my business and was one of my greatest fans. Jolee was my personal, one-woman public relations department.

Not everyone needs or wants the cookie, but they love you and will support you and be your public relations department. My longtime friend Jolee is a case in point.

Relating to a Group or an Audience

Professionals create trust, belief, influence, and rapport before they start their presentation.

Over the years, I have been criticized for not having presentation notes or a strict agenda. I was told that I should have it all planned out with a checklist to make sure I had covered the business, the product, the compensation plan, and so on. The accepted practice for some was to tell the audience everything in order to get the whole big picture at one sitting. This is just not the way I do things.

Acknowledging the audience and how they may be thinking and feeling is always my top priority, and this means I have to go with the flow. I start out by being sensitive to the people who are there and acknowledging that half of them don't want to be there. They were dragged there kicking and screaming by their friends or neighbors, and it's probably a cold winter's night and they really just want to be at home with their feet up. So rather than take them through a cold, preprogrammed process, it's best to make it more entertaining. Smile, tell them that you know they would rather be somewhere else, and thank them for braving the cold to come to the meeting.

I recommend that you always get to the meeting early so that you can mix with the audience before the presentation starts. Introduce yourself and ask them questions; get to know them. Thank them for taking the time to come out and ask who they are with; when you are on stage, if you make eye contact with people you met earlier, smile. Try to include a few of them in your presentation if possible.

Making eye contact with people throughout your presentation is vital, especially for audience members who look totally disinterested. Acknowledge them as real people with feelings and points of view.

Try to touch them with your story. I always found that regardless of what state of mind each person was in at the beginning, telling my story leveled it out so that even if they didn't get all of the pieces of information they wanted, after the meeting they would be asking questions to find out more.

On stage, I would introduce myself as "one of them" who is further along in my journey to freedom. I never presented myself as a heavy hitter, constantly hitting them out of the ballpark.

I believe that my natural sincerity in telling my story helped to thaw some of the more resistant guests and break down their barriers. They knew they could talk to me as simply another person.

Occasionally, I would get into trouble from meeting organizers for turning up without an agenda because they saw it as unprofessional. But this was the way I felt most comfortable and sincere. Developing a relationship with your audience is huge. Sometimes you can best do this at the meeting after the meeting.

The Meeting after the Meeting

Stan Barker taught me the importance of the casual meeting after the formal meeting. Right after the meeting, invite people to go out for a cup of coffee. This is the next meeting, and it is the most important meeting you can have. You can let your hair down and become more personal and personable. Let them know that you've got a teenager and that life's crazy or what's going on in your life. Let them see a little of your world so they can relate.

I wouldn't sell during these meetings, but often, if they really wanted to know more about the business, they would ask me, and that was when they would really start to want to be a part of our warm and friendly group.

I would always try to stay after the formal proceedings, and if the organizer had someone I could take to dinner or hang out with over coffee, I would do that. I wouldn't make the organizer stay, because he or she might have kids to get home to, but of course it was always best if the host could be part of the conversation.

The ability to develop great relationships is a key skill for building your business.

You can't do it alone.

Tapping into Technology

Technology is nothing. What's important is that you have faith in people, that they're basically good and smart, and if you give them tools, they'll do wonderful things with them.

—*Steve Jobs*

Technology is more than social media. Scott has shown me that social media is just one type of technological tool we can use to widen our relationship net; there are many others.

Computers and I are not a natural fit, and it has taken me a while to get a handle on them, but with Scott's help, I now know what I need to know and what it can do to help us build our business. To save you time, we have listed some of the more popular tools available to you.

I am not going into any great in-depth description of how these things work, because you can find millions of resources on the Internet to help you. But try not to get too caught up in the workings. I don't know how my cell phone works, but I use it to get the job done, so rather than getting into the technical details, concentrate on how you can use the technology to help your business.

Social Media

The way we see it, social media refers to Internet sites that are open to the general public and that facilitate social networking:

- Facebook
- Twitter
- LinkedIn
- YouTube
- Pinterest
- Instagram

You might be surprised to learn that in 2013 there were 205 social networking sites.

Facebook is not the only one, but it is the largest, with more than one billion registered users. There are a number of interest-specific Facebook-type sites that could help you connect with like-minded people more quickly. For example, 43Things is a goal-setting and achievement site with three million registered users.

Building relationships via social media is very similar to face-to-face relationship building in that I recommend you take it slowly and get to know people as people rather than as "hot prospects." What you want is to learn a little about what the other person wants in life and for that person to ask you what it is that you do. A great way to pique someone's curiosity is to post photos and comments that reveal a little about your lifestyle.

> *Don't worry if you don't have an exotic car or boat; happy family photos of a day at the beach or a barbecue will do just as well.*

Remember, you are not a sleazy salesperson whose sole objective is pitching the opportunity. You are a Heartfelt Network Marketing professional who listens and cares about the other person and, when appropriate, provides him or her with information he or she might find useful. It is about you sharing not selling, and it is also about giving prospects hope that they may also reach their dreams.

Your Personal Internet

These are the Internet sites and functions where you are in total control of what is published and distributed:

- Your website
- Your blog—people can leave comments, but it is up to you if they are posted.
- Your e-mail campaigns
- Your online trainings
- Your landing pages
- Your webinars
- Your articles

You don't need to have these to build your network marketing business; in fact, most network marketing companies will provide you with a replicated company website that you can personalize and refer your customers and prospects to.

However, these are very helpful if you want to establish yourself as a credible authority in your selected area of business.

The Internet is ideal when it comes to teaching and communicating with vast numbers of people economically and quickly.

If you would like to be on the invite list to our online trainings pease register your interest at:

www.BeyondtheRedDoors.com

or

www.HeartfeltNetworkMarketing.com

We want to help as many people as possible see that they have options and alternative ways to recruit and build a network marketing business.

There is a tendency to think that creating these properties is easy, but unless your background is in technology, I strongly recommend that you concentrate on what you do best and leave the technical stuff to the geeks.

Attracting People to You

You can have anything in life you want, if you will just help enough other people get what they want.

—Zig Ziglar

It is a lot easier to create a relationship with someone who has gone to the effort of contacting you first. The key is for you to create reasons why he or she should want to connect with you. One of the greatest ways to attract people to you is to be of service. Freely provide people with information that is genuinely going to help them achieve their outcome.

Your attraction factor is that you provide valuable information without any strings attached. You are not pitching or selling.

Like I said earlier, work on becoming the person you would love to meet, learn from, and work with. Become known as an educator and authority in your niche; thanks to the Internet, this is much easier and faster today than a few years ago.

Becoming an authority in your niche can best be accomplished by voicing your opinion and giving away insights and educational tips through a wide variety of mediums:

- Blog posts

- Constructive comments on other people's blogs

- Offers to speak at events for free — you can start by speaking at your local mother's group or meet-up group. It doesn't have to be on stage in front of hundreds of people, but that is most likely where you are headed.

- Articles that focus on your niche for your local newspaper or Internet sites

- Short videos on YouTube — they can be as short as thirty seconds; in fact, the shorter the better. Just focus on one little tip at a time.

If you don't know where to start, just think of some of the problems and lessons you have learned so far and write about those. You will be surprised how many others faced the same issues and will appreciate your insights. It doesn't matter how new to your niche you are. In fact, if you are just starting out, you already see the path with newbie eyes, and other newbies will relate to you very quickly.

What matters is that you are passionate and focused and willing to stand up and freely help others.

Join groups that focus on your niche or pet passion and get involved. Don't sit on the sidelines. Jump into the game and voice your opinions and point of view. Over a period of time, other members will look to you as their go-to person and follow your lessons and advice.

A great example of this is a young woman who is involved with a number of Internet forums and blogs that focus on adoption and the issues adoptive parents face. Sadly, there came a time when her family was faced with bankruptcy and foreclosure on their home. They had several adopted children and what appeared to be no way out—until she was introduced to network marketing. With no previous networking experience, she was able to turn her life around within six months. They earned in excess of $100,000 within six months because she found a way out and immediately started telling all her pals on the forums and in the blogs about how she was solving their financial disaster. She didn't ask them to join her. She told her story, and because of her credibility with the group, it didn't take long for other adoptive parents to ask for specifics about the networking company she was building with—and the rest is history.

I personally know many men and women who have similar heartwarming stories, and each one is inspiring and gives hope to us all.

People are attracted to others who are inspiring, helpful, and fun. The only agenda necessary is the desire to genuinely help others and, in so doing, help yourself.

STOP pitching and START teaching.

Having Fun on the Way

People rarely succeed unless they have fun in what they are doing.

—Dale Carnegie

It is important to make it fun. You probably have a serious day job, and the last thing you need is a serious part-time job. No one is forcing you to do this. You are your own boss, and you make the rules. You can make it as serious or as much fun as you wish.

Joining with a friend is a great way to get started. You have someone to talk to who understands what you are doing, and you have someone to laugh along with you.

I started network marketing with my longtime friend Joni. We first met when Joni managed a weight-loss center, and I was running my home hair salon. She always booked her hair appointments for the end of the day so we could spend time together and laugh about the week that was, and over time we became family friends.

Joni has an effervescent, positive energy and is great fun to be around. We often talked about how much fun it would be to work together, but at the time neither of us saw it happening anytime soon.

Our network marketing adventure started when Joni coerced me into listening to a network marketing tape and then dragged me along to a local network marketing meeting. Up to that point, my only experiences with network marketing had been negative. Joni and I were friends, and I loved being around her, so I followed along in spite of my deeply held conviction that all network marketers were sneaky and self-centered.

During the meeting, I realized that network marketing had the potential to be my ticket to freedom. I turned to Joni, thanked her for convincing me to join her, and declared out loud that I could do this.

The very next week, we borrowed money and traveled together to the company meeting. It was exciting being in a room full of people who were energized and excited about life and what they were doing.

We were so fired up that we wrote a song on the first night to the tune of "New York, New York." We were having such a great time singing that a bunch of other members joined us in the elevator, and we went up and down singing our song. The energy and fun was contagious. Everyone who stepped into our elevator left singing our song.

I wish I remembered all the words, but I remember how it began:

You're at the start of it, the very heart of it.

It was electric, and I recruited my first two team members that night— my mother and my aunt. After they signed up, we called them back and sang our song to them over the phone. I think our team grew and gelled so quickly because of our enthusiasm and fun. Everybody liked our team, because we were always having more fun than the others.

Joni and I fell in love with network marketing and our first company. This was fun. We had a blast mixing with like-minded happy and motivated people. We attended every big event, which meant new clothes, new hairdos, special parties, new friends, new places, travel, and new lessons. We were mixing with successful people who constantly reassured us that we had what it took to get to the top, and this kind of support and encouragement was exciting.

We supported each other but built our own teams. We shared books on personal development and sales training and often shared the cost of travel and events. One time we decided at the last minute to go to an event in Idaho and ended up in a no-star hotel. It was so bad the sheets had crusty bits on them, so we slept standing up, but the event and the people made up for everything. The story about sleeping standing up had everyone in tears with laughter.

In Spokane, we were still running on cheap, and in one hotel we could smell the cigarette smoke from the room below. It was terrible. All of a sudden, Joni turned to me and asked what we were doing. We were earning eight to nine thousand dollars a month—we could afford a real hotel, but we were having so much fun learning and doing that we forgot to smell the roses as we were zooming by.

The best piece of advice I was given years ago was that it is no fun going to the party by yourself.

Remember, network marketing is in addition to your regular daily job, so make it fun. You call the shots. This is an option, and no one is forcing you to do it, so why not make it fun? You have nothing to lose and everything to gain while making your dreams come true.

Section IV

ACKNOWLEDGEMENT

Writing this book helped me remember why I fell in love with this profession from the very beginning. It renewed my love for the business of network marketing….. creating new hopes and dreams.

I wish to personally thank the following team for their encouragement, knowledge and expertise throughout this exciting journey of bringing Beyond The Red Doors to life.

Most importantly, my husband **Dr. Scott F. Peterson**, for his vision and his insistence that my story be written. I am forever grateful and truly blessed for his unwavering support, encouragement and love.

Bunker Hill Bradley for his incredible creativity, conceptual vision and artistic talent.

Roselyn Poon for her extraordinary work ethic and systematic approach during the entire project

To my Family and many **Friends**, **Salon Clients** and **Associates**, over the years, who helped me discover and create the freedom that comes from sharing *network marketing* from the *heart*.

Love to all, Shauna

Some of my Favorite Books and Learning Experiences.

Gerber, Michael E. *E-Myth*.

Johnson, Spencer. *Who Moved My Cheese?*

Kiyosaki, Robert T. *Cash Flow Quadrant*.

Kiyosaki, Robert T. *Rich Dad, Poor Dad*.

Leman, Kevin. *The Birth Order Book*.

Maxwell, John C. *Put Your Dream to the Test: 10 Questions that Will Help You See It and Seize It*.

Schwartz, David J. *The Magic of Thinking Big*.

Landmark Education—first part—*The Forum*

Keirsey, David. *Please Understand Me, II*

Tom "Big Al" Schreiter books, CDs and Training; *www.Fortunenow.com*

Art Jonak's Annual Mastermind. *www.MastermindEvent.com*

Ziglar. *www.Ziglar.com*

Direct Selling World Alliance
Co-Founders-Grace and Nickie Keohohou. *www.DSWA.org*

Disclaimer

All Rights Reserved. No part of this book may be reproduced in any form or by any means without prior written permission from the author or publisher except for brief quotations embodied in critical essay, article, or review. These articles and/or views must state the correct title and contributing author of this book by name. Limit of Liability/Disclaimer of Warranty: While the publisher and author have used their best efforts in preparing this book, they make no representations or warranties with respect to the accuracy or completeness of the contents of this book and specifically disclaim any implied warranties of merchantability or fitness for a particular purpose. No warranty may be created or extended by sales representatives or written sales materials. The advice and strategies contained herein may not be suitable for your situation. You should consult with a professional where appropriate. Neither the publisher nor author shall be liable for any loss of profit or any other commercial damages, including but not limited to special, incidental, consequential, or other damages. Earnings Disclaimer: the publisher and author make no implications, warranties, promises, suggestions, projections, representations, or guarantees with respect to future prospects or earnings. Any earnings or income statements, or any earnings or income examples, are only estimates of what it could be possible to earn. There is no assurance you will do as well as stated in any examples. If you rely upon any figures provided, you must accept the entire risk of not doing as well as the information provided. There is no assurance that any prior successes or past results as to earnings or income will apply, nor can any prior successes be used as an indication of your future success or results from any of the information, content, or strategies. Any and all claims or representations as to income or earnings are not to be considered as "average earnings."

While the techniques and approaches suggested may have worked for others, no one can guarantee that they will work for you. We sincerely hope though that the ideas presented here will assist you in developing a strong and profitable business.

.

Made in the USA
Middletown, DE
05 July 2015